CONTENTS

KU-074-866

Hugh Baird College
T55438

A Guide to Practical Scaffolding

The Construction and Use of Basic Access Scaffolds

HUGH BAIRD COLLEGE
LIBRARY AND LEARNING CENTRES

Fully updated in line with the Work at Height Regulations 2005 and BS EN 12811-1.

CE 509

Published by ConstructionSkills, Bircham Newton, King's Lynn, Norfolk PE31 6RH

© **Construction Industry Training Board 1985**

The Construction Industry Training Board, otherwise known as
CITB-ConstructionSkills and ConstructionSkills, is a registered charity (Charity
Number: 264289)

First published 1985
Revised 1988
Revised 1991
Revised 1997
Revised 2005

ISBN: 978 0 90202 991 0

CLASS

690.22 COTU

ACQ

2.7.05

T3543b

Acknowledgement
ConstructionSkills wishes to express its appreciation and thanks for the valuable
contribution made by members of the National Association of Scaffolding Contractors
in preparing this book for publication.

CITB-ConstructionSkills is a partner in ConstructionSkills and from now on you will see
more and more of our products and services branded ConstructionSkills. To find out
why and what this means to you, please visit www.cskills.org

ConstructionSkills has made every effort to ensure that the information contained
within this publication is accurate. Its content should be used as guidance material and
not as a replacement for current regulations or existing standards.

All rights reserved. No part of this publication may be reproduced, stored in a retrieval
system or transmitted in any form or by any means, electronic, mechanical,
photocopying, recording or otherwise, without the prior permission in writing from
ConstructionSkills.

Introduction

With the introduction of the Work at Height Regulations 2005, there is now one set of all-embracing regulations that covers work at height in all industries and in all places of work. Duty holders under the regulations include employers, the self-employed and 'persons in control', such as premises and facilities managers. The regulations have brought about a change in the way in which work at height, including scaffolding, will be planned and carried out. However, due to the very nature of scaffolding, it will not be possible to eliminate work at height, and so the requirements of the regulations need to be understood clearly.

The requirements of the regulations regarding guard-rails will affect both the manner in which a scaffold is erected and the use of safety harnesses. The NASC guide SG:4 2005 (*Preventing Falls in Scaffolding and Falsework*) details the industry requirements for the use of safety harnesses. This is not, therefore, dealt with in this book.

The regulations also require that strength and stability calculations be carried out for all but the generally recognised standard configurations of scaffolds, and that, depending on the complexity of the scaffold, there should be a plan for the assembly, use and dismantling of the scaffold drawn up by a competent person.

It is not the purpose of this book to deal with the calculations or other matters that require input from scaffold design engineers. However, the advice given throughout this book complies with the requirements of the Work at Height Regulations and any guidance so far issued by the Health and Safety Executive.

Another significant change is the withdrawal of British Standard 5973:1993 (*Code of Practice for Access and Working Scaffolds and Special Scaffold Structures in Steel*) and its replacement by BS EN 12811-1 (*Temporary Work Equipment. Part 1. Scaffolds – Performance Requirements and General Design*). The withdrawal of BS 5973 was necessary as it was not compatible with the new standard.

The main differences between the two are the calculation methods for stress and loading; the design requirements for ties, ledger bracing and plan bracing; and wind calculations, which, together, will affect both the designers and erectors of scaffolds.

Whereas BS 5973 gave much useful and practical advice on a whole range of issues, this is not all covered or repeated within BS EN 12811-1. Because the contents of BS 5973 were regarded as the industry standard and as 'best practice', they are used in this book where they do not conflict with BS EN 12811-1 or any other guidance.

The National Access and Scaffolding Confederation (NASC) has published TG20:05 (*Guide to Good Practice for Scaffolding with Tubes and Fittings*), which is technical guidance on the use of BS EN 12811-1, and which reiterates much of the useful information from BS 5973. Throughout this publication the advice given follows that of the NASC. Whereas the NASC guide and this book set out what may be regarded as best industry or best practice, clients may at times require even higher standards.

Part 1

Basic Scaffolding

1. SOME COMMON SCAFFOLDING DEFINITIONS

Over the years, scaffolders in different parts of the UK have evolved their own terminology – their own use of particular names for the various types of scaffold and scaffold fittings in common use. This chapter briefly explains the common names of the basic components of scaffolding, where they are placed in the structure and the job they do. At the end of this book you will find a longer glossary of the terminology used in the industry.

Standards (also known as uprights) are the vertical tubes that carry the entire load to the ground. Each standard should have a *base plate* that, by spreading the load, prevents the end of the tube from sinking into the ground.

The base plate is made from steel and has a central shank for locating the tube. Sometimes the base plate is nailed or pinned to a *sole board* to prevent lateral movement, particularly if no *foot tie or kicker lift* is employed.

The sole board or sole plate is necessary component (particularly on soft ground) to spread the weight over a greater area. This is usually made of timber but, on occasions, may be made of concrete or metal.

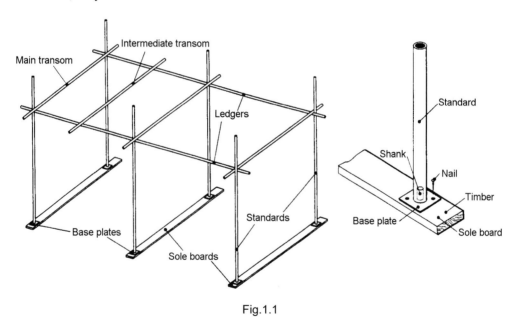

Fig.1.1

Ledgers are the horizontal tubes that connect and support the standards and that act as supports for *transoms*. These usually run in the direction of the larger dimension of the scaffold. The vertical spaces (or distances) between the ledgers are governed by the use for which the scaffold is intended.

The **main transoms** are placed horizontally at right angles across the ledgers, adjacent to each pair of standards, or they are connected directly to each pair of standards. They hold both rows of standards in position, they help to make the scaffold more rigid and they also act as scaffold board supports. They are usually installed in the direction of the smaller dimension of the scaffold.

Intermediate transoms are placed across the ledgers between the main transoms, and they act as scaffold board supports (these are sometimes called 'board bearers').

Cross or ledger braces are essential to the rigidity of the structure and they are placed diagonally across the ledgers, adjacent to alternate pairs of standards. Cross braces are normally fitted directly on to the standards. Ledger braces are fitted to ledgers.

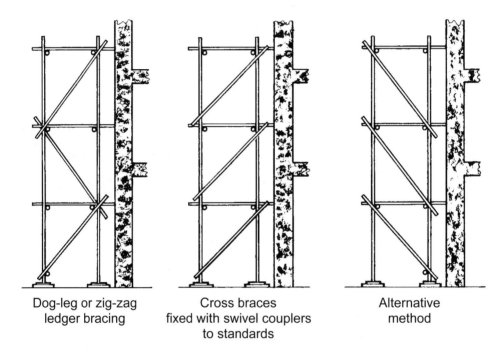

Dog-leg or zig-zag
ledger bracing

Cross braces
fixed with swivel couplers
to standards

Alternative
method

Fig. 1.2

A **facade or sway brace** is a tube fixed to the face of the scaffold to stop the scaffold swaying. It should run from the base to the full height of the scaffold at an angle of between 35° and 55°, and it should be fixed at the base and at every lift level, either to the standards or the ends of the transoms. Facade or sway bracing should be fitted every five bays (or fewer) along the scaffold.

A wide variety of **scaffold couplers** are available, and their use and maintenance depend upon the type of fitting and its application. All fittings should be lightly oiled and kept free from rust (a description of these items and an explanation of their use can be found in Chapter 3). An example of scaffold couplers in use is shown in Fig. 1.3.

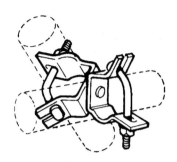

Swivel coupler

Fig. 1.3

Joint pins (or **expanding spigots**) are used to connect tubes end to end. The joint pin (spigot) is inserted into the ends of the tubes and the centre bolt is tightened, which causes the two parts of the spigot to expand and grip the inside of the tubes.

This fitting should *not* be used in positions where it will be subject to bending or tension.

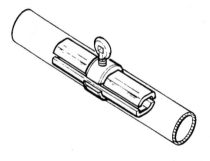

Joint pin (or expanding spigot)

Fig. 1.4

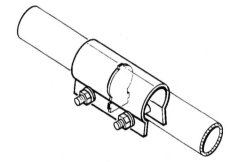

Sleeve coupler

Fig. 1.5

Sleeve couplers, generally called sleeves, are also used to connect tubes end to end. This fitting has a resistance to bending that is at least equal to any tube. It has a safe working tension of 315 kg.

Standard spacing (or **bay length**) is the distance between standards. It is measured along the face of the scaffold.

Foot ties, **foot lifts** or **kicker lifts** are the ledgers and transoms that are fixed near to the bottom of standards, at approximately 150 mm from the ground.

Lift height or **ledger spacing** is the distance between ledgers, measured up the face of the scaffold.

Base lift or **first lift** is the first lift above ground level, other than the foot tie or kicker lift.

Scaffold width is the distance between standards, measured at the shortest point. This is also known as the board width.

Note: Additional terminology is introduced throughout the book and explained as necessary.

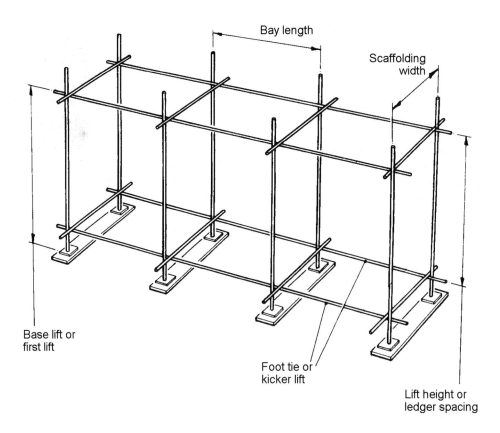

Fig. 1.6
(bracing has been omitted for clarity)

4

2. BASIC SCAFFOLD REQUIREMENTS

The Work at Height Regulations require that strength and stability calculations are made for all scaffolds, unless they have already been done for a previous scaffold of the same design or if it is a scaffold with a generally recognised standard configuration (such as a basic putlog or an independent scaffold).

This book does not cover strength and stability or design issues and calculations; rather, it is concerned with the erection of generally recognised and commonly used scaffold structures in the industry.

The primary reason for erecting a scaffold is to support a working platform. Most construction work involves operating at heights that cannot be reached from the ground or from other parts of the building. Where work has to take place at height, employers must comply with the requirements of the Work at Height Regulations 2005, and must provide a working place or platform that is a safe and convenient means of access and egress.

No scaffold may be erected, altered or dismantled except under the supervision of a competent and experienced person, and by persons who have received specific and appropriate training in the operation, and the precautions, to be taken. Scaffolds erected or altered by people who are not competent, or who have no knowledge or experience, are liable to be dangerous and unsafe.

Scaffolds must be rigid, built of sound materials on good foundations and be well secured to the building or structure. In public places, scaffolds must be well lit or have warning lights fitted at their base. Warning notices must be displayed on incomplete scaffolds, and precautions must be taken to ensure that no unauthorised persons (particularly children and other members of the public) can gain access to the scaffold at any time.

Fig. 2.1

In this introduction to scaffolding requirements, reference will be made to the various critical aspects of scaffolds. Each subject is dealt with in greater detail in separate chapters of this book, but a summary of each subject is given below.

MATERIALS

The materials used to build a scaffold must be in good condition. Steel items should be free from rust, and fittings should be well serviced and free from excessive oil or grease, which may cause the fitting to slip.

Boards should be clean and in good condition. The ends should be bound or nail-plated, and should not be split, warped or twisted. Scaffold boards should not be painted or treated in such a way to conceal defects.

Other materials, such as ropes, gin wheels and ladders, must be in a sound, serviceable condition. All scaffolding materials must be inspected by an experienced and competent person *before use,* and unsound and unserviceable materials clearly marked and removed from the site.

FOUNDATIONS

Every scaffold structure must be 'well founded'. This foundation must be capable of carrying the imposed load for the entire lift of the scaffold. On hard surfaces, such as steel or concrete, standards may be placed directly on the surface. On other surfaces, base plates and sole boards must be used to spread the load. The ground beneath the sole board must be level and properly compacted. Fig. 2.2 shows the minimum requirements for bases to suit a range of ground conditions.

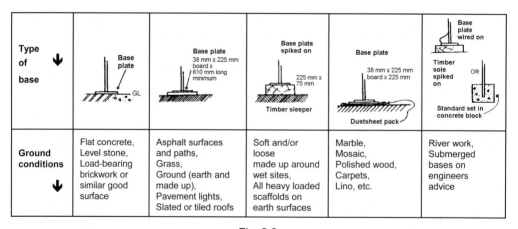

Type of base ↓	Base plate	Base plate 38 mm x 225 mm board x 610 mm long minimum	Base plate spiked on 225 mm x 75 mm Timber sleeper	Base plate 38 mm x 225 mm board x 225 mm Dustsheet pack	Base plate wired on Timber sole spiked on OR Standard set in concrete block
Ground conditions ↓	Flat concrete, Level stone, Load-bearing brickwork or similar good surface	Asphalt surfaces and paths, Grass, Ground (earth and made up), Pavement lights, Slated or tiled roofs	Soft and/or loose made up around wet sites, All heavy loaded scaffolds on earth surfaces	Marble, Mosaic, Polished wood, Carpets, Lino, etc.	River work, Submerged bases on engineers advice

Fig. 2.2

THE SCAFFOLD FRAME

The framework of a scaffold is built from metal tubes of varying lengths, joined together with a variety of couplers or clips (commonly called fittings). The actual design and shape of the structure will depend on the type and intended purpose of the scaffold and the load it is expected to bear. This chapter is only concerned with those features of the structural framework common to most scaffolds.

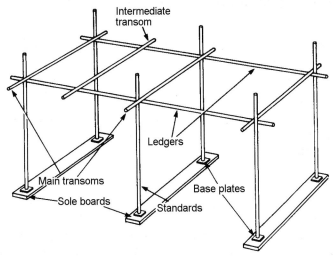

Fig. 2.3

Standards

Standards are the vertical element of the scaffold framework and, as such, they carry the weight of the structure and its load. Standards must be vertical.

The *spacing* of standards is determined by the intended use of the scaffold, and the distance between the spacings is reduced as the expected load increases. Table 2.1 (page 14) (reproduced from TG20:05 with permission of the National Access and Scaffolding Confederation (NASC)) gives details of the maximum *bay length* (standard spacing) for different types of scaffold, the most common being 2.1 m for a general-purpose scaffold. This is reduced to 1.8 m for a heavy-duty scaffolds and for scaffolds being used to carry out masonry and stonework.

The *width* of the working platform, and the distance between the front and back rows of standards, is determined by the purpose for which the scaffold is intended, with a minimum width of 600 mm. This is usually expressed in terms of 'the number of boards wide' – for example, a four-board scaffold would usually require a width spacing of 870 mm from the centre to centre of each standard. This measurement would only vary to accommodate different types of couplers.

Note: The minimum width of 600 mm is a requirement in the Construction (Health, Safety and Welfare) Regulations 1996. These regulations are currently being reviewed, and this minimum width may not appear in any new or revised regulations.

The joints in standards should be staggered – that is, joints should not occur at the same level in adjacent standards. Joints can be made with spigots, but they can also be strengthened with lapped tubes or sleeve couplers, depending on the load.

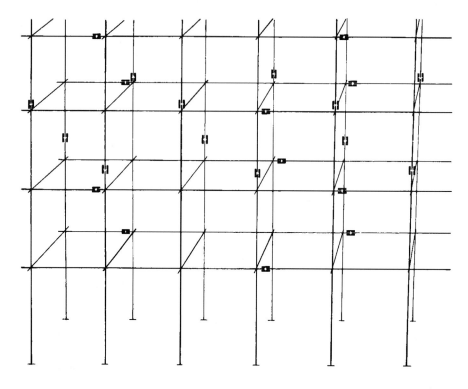

Fig. 2.4

All joints should be staggered and kept as close as possible to the node point (the junction of standard and ledger) as practicable.

Ledgers

Ledgers are the main horizontal tubes, and they provide lateral support to the structure. They must be level and fixed to the inside of standards with right-angle, load-bearing couplers. The vertical distance (lift height, ledger to ledger) will vary depending on the intended use of the scaffold; however, the maximum height for a walk-through scaffold should be 2 m to give a clear headroom of 1.75 m. Where access for the public or others is required under the first (or base) lift, on the other hand, the lift height can be up to a maximum of 2.7 m.

Ledgers should be joined with sleeve couplers, but internal joint pins (spigots) may be used if the joint is within 300 mm of a standard. Internal joint pins should be as close as possible to the point at which the ledger is fixed to the standard. They should never be more than one third of the bay width from a standard. All joints must be staggered.

The kicker lift or foot tie should be set approximately 150 mm above ground level, except where this is impossible for reasons of access. The kicker lift or foot tie is normally used on heavy-duty or long-term scaffolds only, or where there is a possibility that standards could be displaced through low-level impact.

Care should be taken with kicker lifts so that they do not become trip hazards. Signs conforming to the Health and Safety (Safety Signs and Signals) regulations and/or a guard-rail at the appropriate height (or a barrier) may be needed to prevent persons tripping on the kicker lift.

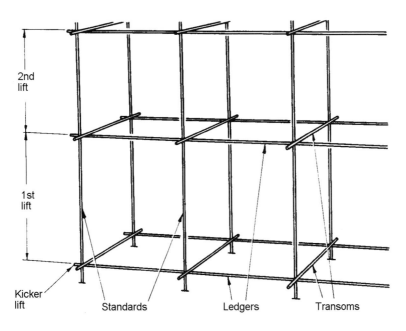

Fig. 2.5

Putlogs and transoms

Main transoms are fixed, either directly across to every pair of standards, using right-angle couplers, or laid across and fixed to ledgers with putlog couplers. In this case, transoms should be fixed as close as possible, but never more than 300 mm from each pair of standards. Main transoms hold the two rows of standards in position, are an integral part of the structure and must not be removed unless expert advice is sought.

A putlog is the name given to the horizontal tube used when there is only one row of standards. One end of the putlog is fixed to the scaffold in the same way as a transom, while the other end is supported directly by the structure against which the scaffold is being erected. Where new brickwork is being built, the putlog will have a flattened end, laid horizontally in the joints between the bricks.

Transoms or putlogs should never be laid more than 1.2 m apart when used as supports for 38 mm scaffold boards, or 2.6 m apart when used for 50 mm boards. The *length* of the putlog or transoms will be determined by the *width* of the proposed platform, which in turn will be decided by the use for which it is intended. The minimum width of working platforms should be 600 mm.

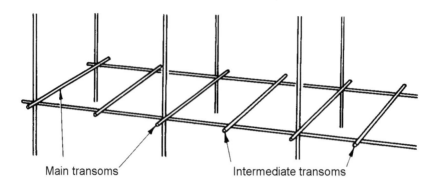

Main transoms   Intermediate transoms

Fig. 2.6

Intermediate transoms

If the lift is to be boarded over as a working platform, *intermediate transoms* will be required to support the boards. These are fixed across ledgers with putlog couplers, normally in the centre of each bay, although additional intermediate transoms may be required to support short boards. They may safely be removed and used elsewhere in the structure when the platform is no longer required.

Ties

Ties are, in many cases, critical to the safety of a scaffold. To ensure that the scaffold framework cannot move away from, or towards, the structure, the framework must be stabilised. This is normally achieved by securing the scaffold framework to the building with positive two-way ties (ties are discussed in detail in Chapter 5).

Ties must not be removed, except by an experienced and competent scaffolder, who must ensure that the stability of the scaffold is not jeopardised. If any ties are to be removed for access or for any other purpose, alternative ties must first be fixed to maintain the stability of the scaffold.

Ties must be checked at regular intervals, and checked again *before* dismantling.

Braces

All scaffold structures must be braced in both directions. *Facade* (or sway braces) should be fitted along the outer face of the scaffold, from the base to the full height of the structure. In the case of non-standard or large scaffold structures, the design will show the requirements for bracing, which will depend on the scaffold's intended use and the information given in NASC TG20:05.

Facade bracing can be continuous across the full face of the scaffold or it may be placed across a number of bays in a zig-zag (dog-leg) fashion. Joints in facade braces must be made with sleeve couplers. If joint pins (spigots) are used, each joint must be strengthened with a lapped tube.

Braces must be connected to the standards at every lift using swivel couplers, or to the ends of transoms with right-angle couplers, in which case the transom itself must be fixed with right-angle couplers.

Ledger braces connect the front standards to the rear standards and are generally placed at every other pair of standards and at every lift. As free access through the scaffold has to be provided for the other trades who are working on the site, ledger bracing has, in some cases, to be taken out to provide this access. The erection plan or the scaffold design engineer will say which ledger's braces have to be removed and whether additional bracing or ties are required elsewhere. All the braces form an integral part of the scaffold structure and must not be removed without authority, and then only by a competent scaffolder.

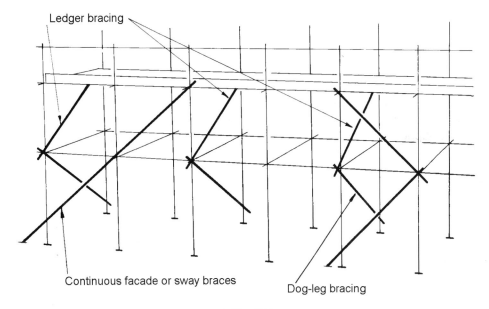

Fig. 2.7

WORKING PLATFORM

As previously noted, the primary purpose of a scaffold is to provide support for a temporary working platform. The law requires that all places of work must be safe for the users and must not expose anyone to any risk to their safety or health (i.e. other trades people and members of the public).

Working platforms must be close boarded and must be fitted with guard-rails and toe-boards (including stop ends). If materials are stacked on the platform above the height of the toe-board, a suitable barrier (such as a brick guard) must be used to prevent the materials from falling off.

The *width* of the working platform must be a minimum of 600 mm. The uses for which these platforms are designed are given in the tables at the end of this chapter (see pages 14 and 15). These tables have been reproduced from TG20:05 with the permission of the NASC.

A working platform must be provided with a means of access that is safe and that does not present any risk. This is usually a ladder. The ladder must be secured properly and be long enough to extend above the working platform to provide a secure handhold when getting on to the working platform (this is usually taken to mean 1 m or five rungs), unless other adequate handholds are provided. Landing areas must be fitted with guard-rails and toe-boards and should be kept clear (see Chapters 6 and 7).

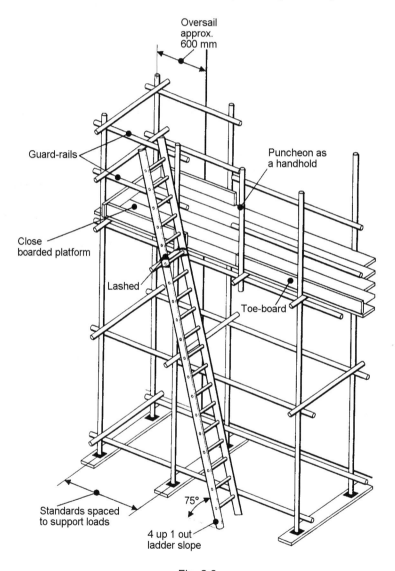

Fig. 2.8

12

LOADS ON SCAFFOLDS

Care must be taken that the load does not exceed the permissible limits (see Table 2.1 on page 14). The materials should be distributed as evenly as possible, and heavy items, such as bricks, should be stacked near to the standards.

INSPECTION

Under the Work at Height Regulations 2005, scaffolds and scaffold working platforms are 'work equipment', and the regulations require that a scaffold must not be used until it has been inspected by a competent person. This will normally be the 'hand over' inspection. If the scaffold is being used for construction work within the meaning of the regulations, and a person could fall two metres or more, then the 'user' of the scaffold must ensure that the scaffold has been inspected by a competent person within the previous seven days. In the case of mobile scaffolds or working platforms, these must also have been inspected on site within the previous seven days. Details of the inspection must be recorded.

Although the regulations do not define a 'competent person', for the purposes of scaffold inspection this can be taken to mean a person who has practical and theoretical knowledge of scaffolding, together with actual experience of what they are to examine or inspect, so that they are able to detect any errors, defects, faults or weaknesses in the scaffold. It is the purpose of the examination or inspection to discover and to assess the importance of any such faults and to act accordingly.

The particulars that should be included in the inspection report include the following:

1. The name and address of the person for whom the inspection was carried out.

2. The location of the work (the scaffold(s)) inspected.

3. A description of the work equipment inspected.

4. The date and time of the inspection.

5. Details of any matter identified that could give rise to a risk to the health or safety of any person.

6. Details of any actions taken as a result of any matter identified in point 5.

7. Details of any further action considered necessary.

8. The name and position of the person making the report.

Table 2.1: Load classes for access and working scaffolds made from tube and fittings

Load class	Duty	Likely use of platform	Uniformly distributed load on platform kN/m²	Max. number of platforms in use (udl kN/m²)	Max. bay length m	Max. spacing board transoms mm	Max. number of boards	Width class
1	Inspection and very light duty	Inspection, painting, stone cleaning, light cleaning and access	0.75	One Full (0.75) and One 50% (0.375)	2.7	1,200	3	WO6
2	Light duty	Plastering, painting, stone cleaning, glazing and pointing	1.50	One Full (1.50) and One 50% (0.75)	2.4	1,200	4	WO9
3	General purpose	General building work including brickwork, window and mullion fixing, rendering and plastering	2.00	One Full (2.00) and One 50% (1.00)	2.1	1,200	5	WO9
3i			2.00		2.1	1,200	4 + 1	WO9
4	Heavy duty	Masonry work, concrete block work, and very heavy cladding	3.00	One Full (3.00) and One 50% (1.50)	1.8	900	5	WO9
4i			3.00		1.8	900	4 + 1	WO9

Notes to Table 2.1:

i) Load classes 3i and 4i have been introduced into this NASC Guide to identify scaffolds with one board on the inside of the inside standard.

ii) Platform units for scaffolds of load class 1 shall be capable of supporting class 2 loads.

Table 2.2: Widths of access working platforms

Purpose [1]	Minimum clear width mm	Minimum number of 225 mm nominal width boards mm	Effective width of boarded platform for loading calculations [2] mm
Working platforms for men without materials or only for the passage of materials	600	3 boards	705
For men and materials provided there is 430 mm left clear for the passage of men or 600 mm if barrows are used	800	4 boards	930
For carrying trestles or other similar higher platforms	1,050	5 boards or 4 + 1 board	1,155 1,155
For use in dressing or roughly shaping stone [3]	1,300	6 boards	1,350

[1] Where internal ladders are incorporated the minimum width may be 430 mm, i.e. two boards

[2] Effective width as defined in BS EN 12811-1 includes a 30 mm allowance for toe-board

[3] These scaffolds should be specially designed

Table 2.3: Maximum and target span of scaffold boards

Board specification	Thickness		Transom spacing (span of board)			Board overhang	
			Target span		Maximum span		
	Nominal	Tolerance	Span	Tolerance		Minimum	Maximum
	mm	mm	mm	mm	mm	mm	mm
NASC TG5	38	± 2	1,200	+100	–	50	150
BS 2482-1 38-1.2 m 38-1.5 m [1]	38 38	± 2 ± 2	1,200 1,200	+100 +100	– –	50 50	150 150
BS 2482-2	50 63	± 3 ± 3	– –	– –	2,600 3,250	50 50	200 250

[1]   Board properties verified by machine stress grading

Reproduced with permission from NASC guide TG20:05.

3. MATERIALS

Scaffolding materials consist primarily of tubes, boards and couplers. Additional items (such as ropes, gin wheels and ladders) are covered in separate chapters of this book. The care and maintenance of tubes, boards and fittings are of prime importance as they affect both safety and profitability.

All scaffolding materials must be inspected before use by a competent and experienced scaffolder and any unserviceable items discarded. Unserviceable items should be clearly marked and removed from the site to prevent their accidental use.

SCAFFOLD TUBES

Tubes and fittings are manufactured to BS EN 39:2001 *(Loose Steel Tube for Tube and Fitting Scaffolds)*.

There are three main types of tube in common use:

- Black steel tubes.

- Galvanised steel tubes.

- Aluminium alloy tubes.

Black steel and galvanised steel tubes have the same dimensions, but galvanised tubes are more resistant to corrosion. The common dimensions for type-4 tubes are as follows:

- Outside diameter, 48.3 mm.

- Nominal wall thickness, 4.0 mm.

- Weight, 4.4 kg/m.

Type-3 steel tube has a slightly thinner wall thickness of 3.2 mm.

Aluminium tube has the same outside diameter as steel, but it is slightly thicker and much lighter. It is more flexible than steel but not as strong. For this reason aluminium tube should not be used on the same lift as steel tube. However, advantage can be taken of the best characteristics of the two materials by placing aluminium tube on top of steel tube in tall scaffold structures. The common dimensions of aluminium tube are as follows:

- Outside diameter, 48.3 mm.

- Nominal wall thickness, 4.5 mm.

- Weight, 1.7 kg/m.

Aluminium tube is heat tempered during manufacture. Any further heat applied to the tube, therefore, may weaken it.

Lightly corroded tubes should be cleaned with a wire brush and the extent of the damage assessed by a competent and experienced scaffolder. Bent steel tubes may be straightened using a rolling machine, but bent aluminium tube should be discarded.

Inspection

Any scaffold's ability to carry its load is largely dependent on the strength and condition of the tubes used in its construction. Consequently, tubes must be checked to ensure that they are:

- straight
- free from cracks, splits, bad dents and excessive corrosion
- cut square and clean at each end.

Common faults

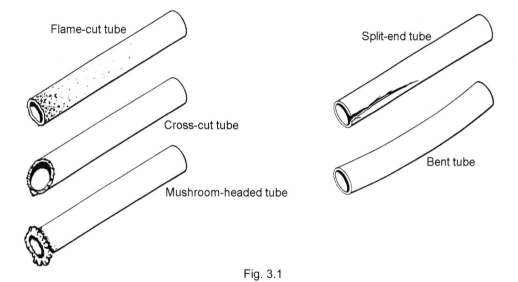

Fig. 3.1

Storage

Scaffold tubes are generally supplied in lengths of 6.4 m. Shorter tubes are available from stock (for example, transoms 1.5 m and 1.8 m in length). Wherever possible, tubes should be sorted according to length and stored in racks with their ends flush. This makes it easier to identify and select tubes of the required length.

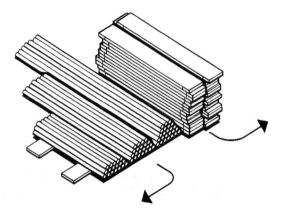

Fig. 3.2

SCAFFOLD BOARDS

Nearly all scaffold boards are manufactured from sawn and seasoned timber. All boards should comply with BS 2482 (*Specification for Timber Scaffold Boards*). This standard identifies the types of wood that may be used in the manufacture of scaffold boards and recommends a method of testing to assess their bending strength. NASC guide TG5 (*Scaffold Board Specification*) follows the British Standard.

Timber boards come in three thicknesses (38 mm, 50 mm and 63 mm) and they are normally 225 mm wide and 3,900 mm long. Shorter boards can be used when necessary. The most common board is 225 mm x 38 mm in cross-section.

Steel decking and laminated boards

A number of firms market stagings made of steel or aluminium and laminated boards. These come in a variety of widths. The safe spans should be quoted in the manufacturer's literature, and timber items should comply with BS 1129 (*Timber Ladders, Steps, Trestles and Lightweight Staging for Industrial Use*). This staging is often used in conjunction with proprietary systems of scaffolding. Portable aluminium ladders, steps, trestles and lightweight stagings are covered by BS 2037.

Identification of boards

Each board should be clearly marked with the following information:

- The British Standard number (BS 2482).
- The supplier's identification mark.

- The letter M or V (which denote machine or visually graded).

- The word 'support', followed by the maximum span in metres over which the board has to be supported, followed by the abbreviation 'max' (for example, BS 2482 AB Co. M support 1.5 max).

This information is normally given on the hoop irons or nail plates which provide board-end protection.

Alternatively, a special identification plate may be used.

Fig. 3.3

Inspection and maintenance

Care should be taken of all the boards in use (for example, overstressing caused by impact loading should not be allowed). Boards being used as ramps or platforms over long spans should be supported regularly, and they should not be placed where vehicular or other loads can be put on them. Boards showing any signs of damage from vehicles, such as tyre marks, should be destroyed.

Scaffold boards should be cleaned, and the hoop irons or nail plates secured or replaced if necessary. Split boards may be cut down or repaired using nail plates, depending on the degree of damage. Cut-outs, burns, oil stains or projecting nails should not be present, and boards that have any of these should be discarded.

Boards should not be painted or treated in any way that may conceal defects, but they can be fireproofed using an approved material.

Common faults

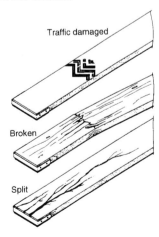
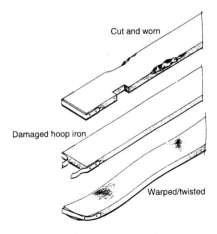

Fig. 3.4

19

Storage

Scaffold boards should be stacked no more than 20 high. The stacks should be separated by short timber battens and should placed on level timbers, off the ground, to protect them from surface water. Boards must be protected from the weather and must have a free circulation of air.

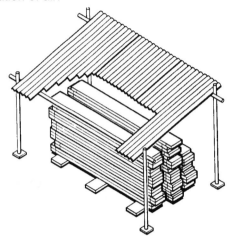

Fig. 3.5
(roof shown cut away for clarity)

SCAFFOLD COUPLERS

Sometimes called scaffold 'fittings', scaffold couplers are designed and tested to British or European standard specifications. Because of the diversity of their design, many fittings achieve higher safe working loads (SWL) than those laid down by the standards, but it would be impossible and improper to quote the different company fittings and their values. All the SWLs and values quoted in this book are those specified by the standards.

Right-angle couplers (also called *doubles*) are always used to connect ledgers to standards. They are designed and tested to achieve a right-angled connection with a minimum safe working load of 635 kg.

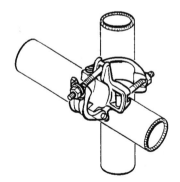

Fig. 3.6

Putlog couplers (also called *clips* and *singles*) are used to connect transoms to ledgers. They are only suitable for light-duty use (hence they are sometimes referred to as being non-load bearing). Putlog couplers must be capable of passing the slip test as specified by the standards.

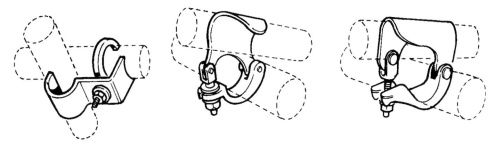

Fig. 3.7

Swivel couplers are used to connect tubes at any angle. Normally, they are used to connect braces to standards and, occasionally, to make parallel joints. Swivel couplers should **never** be used as right-angle couplers.

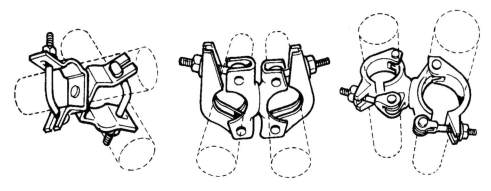

Fig. 3.8

Inspection and maintenance

Scaffold fittings must be inspected by an experienced and competent scaffolder before use. Any broken or damaged fittings should be discarded, as should any with damaged threads. Rusty threads (if they are not defective) should be wire brushed and lightly oiled.

Scaffold fittings should be sorted by type and should be kept clean and dry in strong sacks. The fittings should also be lightly oiled to prevent rust. Each sack should contain only that amount of fittings that can be handled easily – usually no more than 30 fittings per sack. The Manual Handling Operations Regulations put a duty on employers to ensure that their employees are not required to handle excessive weights.

MANAGEMENT OF MATERIALS

Materials must be delivered to the site when required and removed and stored when the job is finished. To ensure that the correct amounts and types of materials arrive at the right place and at the right time needs careful planning and organisation. This planning is normally undertaken by the scaffolding depot where the materials are stored. The day-to-day management of depots is beyond the scope of this book, although it is discussed briefly in Chapter 11.

4. SCAFFOLD FOUNDATIONS

Any structure, whether it is a house or a multistorey block of flats, must have foundations that are capable of carrying the load safely for its entire life. This also applies to scaffolds. The foot of any standard or upright must be adequately founded on a suitable base or base plate to prevent slipping or sinking, or its movement or displacement must be prevented in some other way.

FOUNDATIONS

The foundations for a scaffold must always be adequate to carry and spread the load imposed, both locally at each standard and collectively to carry the whole weight of the scaffold.

It is the responsibility of the scaffold designer and the scaffolder to ensure that the foundations are of adequate strength to support the scaffold and, in practice, this is often done through a consultation between designers, clients and scaffolders.

The foundations for a scaffold must be maintained in a safe condition during the life of the scaffold.

Base plates

Hard surfaces (such as steel and concrete): where there is a sufficient strength and thickness to prevent the scaffold tube penetrating the surface, the uprights of a scaffold may be placed directly on the surface, although it is recommended that base plates should always be used.

Surfaces of intermediate hardness (such as pavements, hard asphalt, timber and flooring): where there is a possibility the standards may deform the surface, base plates should be used at the bottom of each standard.

Sole boards

On any type of flooring or paving that could be penetrated by a standard with a base plate beneath it, or if there is doubt about the surface, the load should be spread further through the use of a sole board of timber or other suitable material.

When a sole board is used, the sole board beneath any one standard should be at least 1,000 cm², with a minimum dimension of 22 cm. If the sole board is of timber, it should not be less than 3.5 cm thick. On sites where the ground is soft or has been disturbed, the total area of each sole board should not be less than 1,700 cm² when it is used under individual standards (e.g. under hoist towers), and not less than 3,400 cm² when combined under two standards. In this case, if the sole board is of timber, it may need to be more than 3.5 cm thick (see Fig. 2.2 on page 6). Heavy-duty scaffolds and poor ground will require stronger foundations.

These are the minimum requirements; in practice they can be interpreted as follows:

- **On firm ground** – 500 mm long x 225 mm x 35 mm.
- **On soft ground** – 765 mm x 225 mm x 35 mm.
- **Under two standards** – 1,550 mm long x 225 mm x 35 mm.

Soil compaction

The soil or ground beneath the sole board should be well compacted and free from irregularities that would make the sole board unstable or poorly bedded. On slopes exceeding 1:10, a check may have to be made by a qualified engineer on the ground's stability before the scaffold is erected.

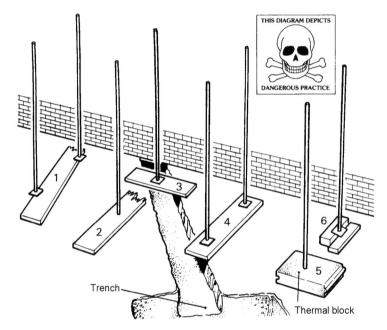

Fig. 4.1

BAD PRACTICE

It is clear in Fig. 4.1 that each standard is wrongly and badly founded (based). Unfortunately, these faults are still occasionally found on construction sites and can cause scaffolds to collapse, resulting in injury or death:

1 The board has not been properly 'bedded'. It is too long and has been struck by a fork-lift or dumper truck, which has knocked it off-centre.

2 The board is too long; it has no base plate.

3 & 4 These were correct until somebody dug the trench! As it is, the edge of the trench could crumble or the boards could bend and possibly break.

5 & 6 These are not proper sole boards. The thermal block (5) will crack and (6) comprises just scrap timber.

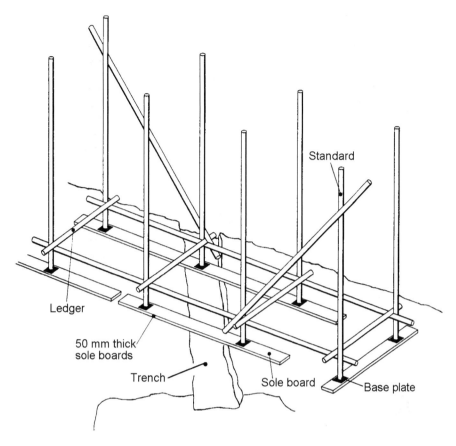

Fig. 4.2

Fig. 4.2 shows the correct method for founding the scaffold shown in Fig. 4.1. Note that facade braces have been added to transfer the loading away from the base of those standards which are near the trench (the fittings have been omitted for clarity).

BASIC RULES

1. The ground must be capable of supporting the scaffold.

2. The sole boards must be capable of spreading the weight of the structure without distortion.

3. Two standards per sole board are better than one.

4. Sole boards placed at right angles to the building must not project too far beyond the face of the scaffold.

5. Sole boards must not be undermined.

6 Sole boards must not become trip hazards.

Heavy-duty foundations

Fig. 4.3 shows a typical arrangement for a multistorey, independent scaffold. Railway sleepers have been set into a shallow bed of concrete with base plates pinned to the sleepers. The standards have been further supported with a kicker lift at the base of the scaffold. All the connections have been made with right-angle couplers directly to the standards for additional rigidity and strength.

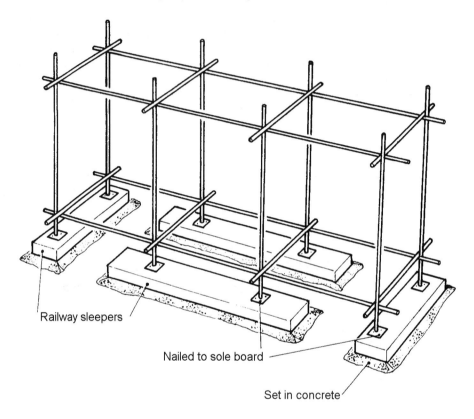

Railway sleepers

Nailed to sole board

Set in concrete

Fig. 4.3
(fittings, braces and intermediate transoms have been left out for clarity)

Before heavy-duty foundations are laid, consideration should be given to any proposed adaptations that may be required during the life of the scaffold because this may affect the position of the sole boards. For instance, it may be necessary to add double standards at the base of the scaffold. In this case sole boards should be placed parallel to the building and should be long enough to accommodate the extra standards. Bridging may be necessary for vehicular access. Sole boards should be placed at right angles to the building at the appropriate places to accommodate this.

Pavement scaffold foundations

Fig. 4.4 identifies some of the problems facing a scaffolder when trying to build (or found) a scaffold on a pavement. Apart from the normal problems, it may be necessary to remove the base-lift braces for public access. Consideration should also be given to the need for additional ties near the base.

The figure shows some of the difficulties that can be avoided with proper planning. If the pavement surface is tarmac, every standard should have a sole board. Sometimes pavement lights may have been covered with tarmac and it is important to check for this. Full-size pavement slabs are normally adequate to take the weight of access scaffolds, but with small paving slabs and block paving, sole boards and base plates are required. Many local authorities also impose other requirements on scaffolds that are built where the public have access, particularly in respect of trip and contact hazards and access for people with disabilities.

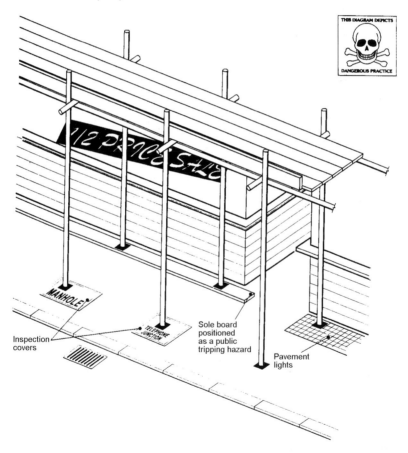

Fig. 4.4

Light-duty access scaffolds can be founded on pavements, without sole boards, provided the pavement is capable of supporting the scaffold (i.e. full-size paving slabs or a continuous concrete paving).

Foundations on sloping ground

Fig. 4.5 is a good example of a well founded scaffold base on sloping ground. The standards are supported by a tie ledger, which is connected to the ends of the transoms with right-angle couplers. Base plates are positioned in the centre of the sole boards, which in turn have been laid in well cut 'steps' in the bank.

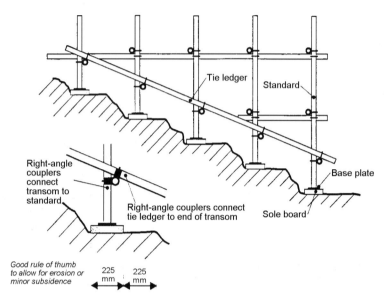

Fig. 4.5
(braces have been omitted for clarity)

Fig. 4.6 gives typical examples of inadequate and unsafe sloping foundations.

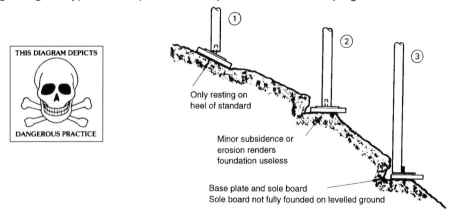

Fig. 4.6

Slopes steeper than 1:10 should be checked for stability by a qualified engineer before the scaffold is erected.

5. TIES

Stability

Scaffolds are often erected to substantial heights and, to ensure the stability of the scaffold, it is necessary to tie them to the adjacent building structure. The system of tubes that prevents movement either towards or away from the structure is referred to as the 'ties'.

GENERAL RULES

Ties usually pass through the facade of the structure and should be secured to the scaffold with load-bearing right-angle couplers, as close to a node point (the junction of the standard and ledger) as possible. In certain cases the tie may not be at right angles to the structure, in which case swivel couplers may be used. At least half the ties should be 'positive', two-way ties – that is, they should prevent movement both towards and away from the building and should not depend on friction (as in the case of a reveal tie – see Fig. 5.5 on page 35) or merely restrict movement in one direction.

It is important to ensure that the building is strong enough to sustain the load that will be transferred to it via the tie. Parapets or decorative architectural features, such as balustrades and railings, are seldom strong enough for this purpose and should not be relied upon.

The tie tube should always be horizontal or slope slightly downwards away from the building, and preferably be attached to both standards, or to both ledgers at a point *not more than* 300 mm from a braced standard.

Where wire or banded ties are used, they should be turned round a node point or otherwise be prevented from slipping along a ledger or upright. This can be achieved by fixing safety couplers either side of the point of attachment, and butt transoms should additionally be used. A butt transom, as its name implies, is a transom that butts hard up against the structure that is being served by the scaffold.

NUMBER AND POSITION OF TIES

BS EN 12811-1 brought about an increase in the number of, and the positioning of, ties and it is the responsibility of the scaffold design engineer to ensure that the requirements of the standard are met in the design.

The number of ties and the positioning of the ties will depend on such factors as the following:

- The intended use of the scaffold and the length of time it will be in position.
- The loadings that will be imposed on the scaffold.
- The overall size, and especially the height, of the scaffold.
- Whether or not it will be sheeted or netted.
- The scaffold's location, its distance from the coast (or sea) and the 'wind factor.

The NASC guide gives details of the maximum safe heights and the class (type) of ties needed for putlog and independent scaffolds, both sheeted and unsheeted, and it is this information scaffold design engineers should use when making their design decisions.

The three classes of ties in the NASC guide are as follows:

- Light duty, with a safe load in pure tension of 3.5 kN.

- Standard, with a safe load in pure tension of 6.1 kN.

- Heavy duty, with a safe load in pure tension of 12.2 kN.

For basic putlog and independent scaffolds, ties must be positioned at every other standard, on every other lift (but with a maximum vertical interval of 4 m) and at top working platform level if the scaffold is sheeted or netted.

It should be remembered that the figures above are the minimum requirements on reasonably standard scaffold, and that it is often necessary or appropriate to put in additional ties.

Basic rules of thumb worth remembering are as follows:

- Space ties every other lift, but not more than 4 m apart, and every other standard along the face of the scaffold.

- Ties should be fixed with load-bearing couplers as close to the node points as possible.

- Avoid the use of reveal ties where possible. At least half the ties on a scaffold must be 'positive'.

- Take full advantage of the structural features of the building, such as pillars, columns, lintels and rebates, to provide the tie with additional strength and stability.

- Make sure the building is strong enough to support the tie and the load imposed on it by the scaffold.

- Do not remove a tie for any reason until the overall stability of the scaffold has been confirmed

For all other scaffolds the number and position of ties will be one of the design factors to be decided by the scaffold design engineer, and as such is outside the scope of this book.

Ties for sheeted scaffolds

Scaffolds fitted with such things as sheeting, tarpaulins or netting will be subjected to extra stress due to wind forces and will therefore require more ties. Special calculations must be made, based on the content of the NASC guide. These should be undertaken by a scaffold design engineer and, thus, again, are outside the scope of this book.

TYPES OF TIE

Ties are often described as being movable and non-movable. Ties that are put in as the scaffold is being built and that are left in place until the scaffold is dismantled are non-movable ties, and these are always to be preferred.

Movable ties are those that, for various reasons, may have to be removed on a temporary basis to allow other work to take place. While a tie is not in place the scaffold is not as secure as it was, and allowance for this must be made at the design stage or alternative arrangements made to ensure the scaffold's stability. Where a scaffold will incorporate movable ties, the design should allow for this.

Through ties

Through ties rely on a tube (the tie tube) passing through any convenient opening in the building (such as a window or door opening) and on being coupled to an inside tube that spans the opening. This inside tube should preferably be vertical, resting on the floor so that it cannot slip, but it may be placed horizontally. If possible, the tie tube should rest on a window sill or other convenient ledge to avoid slipping, but it may be placed under the lintel. The basic principle is to derive as much support and security from the building as possible.

Through ties must be positive, two-way ties to prevent movement both towards and away from the building. Where it is not possible to fix a *bridle tube* (the outer horizontal tube spanning the wall opening; see Fig. 5.1), the adjacent transoms should butt against the outer surface of the wall.

On a putlog scaffold, where the putlogs are required to support boards, a bridle tube is placed near the wall across adjacent putlogs either side of a wall opening. This arrangement can also serve as a through tie by extending a putlog inwards and connecting it to a horizontal (or vertical) tube inside the wall. In this case, load-bearing, right-angle couplers should be used to secure the tie tube, which should pass *below* the ledger. There are two reasons for this. First, right-angle, load-bearing couplers are bulkier than simple putlog couplers and would prevent the scaffold boards from lying flat. Secondly, it is better if the tubes are not used as a direct support for a working platform as the weight and vibration of the platform impose extra stress on the tie tube.

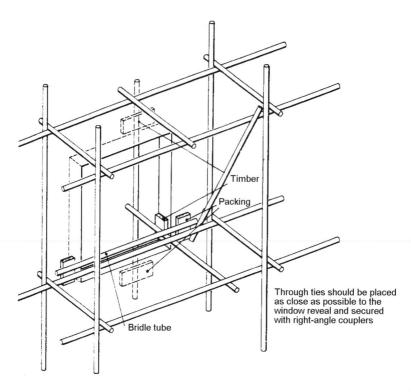

Timber

Packing

Through ties should be placed
as close as possible to the
window reveal and secured
with right-angle couplers

Bridle tube

Fig. 5.1 Through tie
(couplers not shown for clarity)

Box ties

These ties take advantage of a building's physical characteristics and consist of an
assembly of tubes and couplers fixed around convenient columns and other features of
the building. They are wedged where necessary to resist both the inward and outward
pull of the scaffold and to provide additional lateral stability.

Together with through ties, box ties – when properly used – add greatly to the strength
and stability of a scaffold.

Box ties (see Fig. 5.2) should preferably be set at lift level and should be secured to
both inside and outside ledgers on standards unless this is likely to obstruct free
access through the scaffold, in which case they may be fixed to a single inside a
standard. Load-bearing couplers should be used.

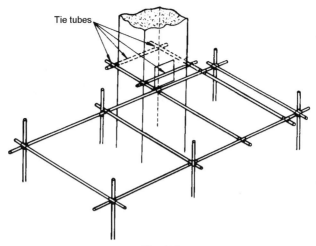

Tie tubes

Fig. 5.2

Lip ties

Where it is not possible to use box ties, lip ties may be used instead. These consist of an L-shaped arrangement of tubes and couplers that hooks behind a convenient part of the building that is of adequate strength. As such they only restrain an outward movement of the scaffold and should therefore be reinforced by an adjacent butting transom or similar arrangement to restrict inward movement. Lip ties contribute little or nothing to the lateral stability of the scaffold, and a sway transom or additional bracing may be required.

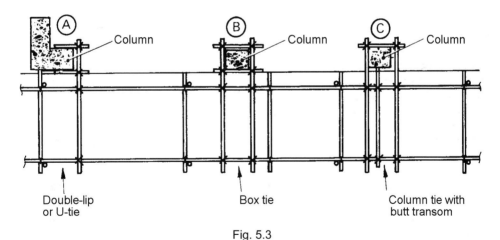

Fig. 5.3

Screw or anchor ties

In some buildings, anchorage points for scaffold ties are built into the fabric of the building during its construction, and a wide variety of screwed plates, sockets and nuts is available for setting into the concrete during pouring. These anchorage points are used for the subsequent maintenance or refurbishment of the building.

However, the older the building, and the longer that such anchorages have been in place, the more they may have deteriorated, and strength or 'pull out' tests may be needed before they are used for scaffold ties. Anchor sockets, ring bolts and other anchorages are also available for fixing into holes drilled into the concrete, stonework or brickwork of the building. It is absolutely essential that proper testing should be carried out to ensure that the design strength of the fixing has in fact been achieved before it is used. Such testing may be carried out by the installer or by an independent tester. When drilling into brick, however, care must be taken to drill into the body of the brick, not near the edge and not into the mortar between bricks as this is unlikely to produce a secure fixing.

With all drilled-in fixings, it is essential that holes are drilled to the depth and diameter specified by the manufacturer and that the correct tools are used for setting expansion anchors.

Before a drilled-in fixing or anchor is used a second time (or reused), advice should be sought as to its continued safety.

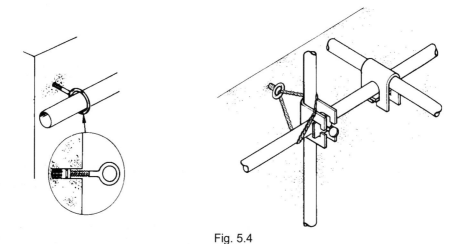

Fig. 5.4

It is important to ensure that the facade material forms an integral part of the building's structure and that it is not merely cladding with little or no actual strength, as is the case with timber-framed housing or system-built structures.

Such things as ring bolts and tie rings, which rely on an expanding wedge to secure the anchor into a predrilled hole, should not be over tightened. Where appropriate the special tool supplied by the manufacturers should be used to fix the anchor, and the ring bolt or other fixing inserted and tightened by hand. Drilled-in ties should be tested before use by a competent scaffolder. The tube or band that passes through the ring will prevent them from becoming unscrewed.

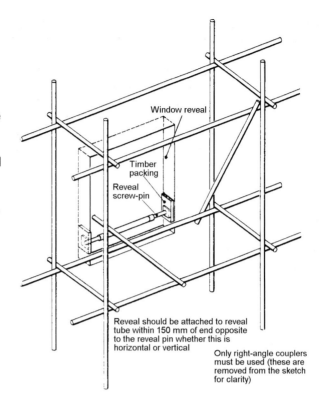

Window reveal

Timber packing

Reveal screw-pin

Reveal should be attached to reveal tube within 150 mm of end opposite to the reveal pin whether this is horizontal or vertical

Only right-angle couplers must be used (these are removed from the sketch for clarity)

Fig. 5.5

Reveal ties

It is not always possible to provide a positive tie, such as a box tie, or to drill the face of a building for screw or anchor ties. In these circumstances, a reveal tie may sometimes be used.

A reveal tie relies on a tube (the reveal tube) that has been wedged tightly between two opposite and parallel faces in the building's structure, such as the opposing sides of a window opening or the underside of a lintel and the sill. The most common device is a threaded bar and nut (called a 'reveal screw pin') which can be adjusted so that the reveal tube assembly expands in the opening, thus gripping it with considerable frictional force. It is usually necessary to use some form of packing at the end of the reveal tube to prevent damage to the building's surface. A 150 mm x 150 mm piece of plywood, 10 mm thick, is usually adequate for this purpose. Excessive packing should be avoided as it may shrink and thus reduce the grip, causing the reveal tube to become loose. The weather may also affect the packing, and so reveal tubes should be checked at regular intervals, especially after any exceptionally wet or hot weather.

The tie tube should be fixed to the reveal tube with a right-angle coupler, as near as possible to the end opposite the reveal pin and, in all cases, within 150 mm of the face of the opening. It should also be fixed to the scaffold in two places with right-angle couplers, as for through ties. Every opportunity should be taken to make use of the building's architectural features (structural not decorative) to provide additional security and stability for the scaffold.

As reveal ties rely entirely on friction, they should also be checked at least once every seven days for tightness. They should not be used on putlog scaffolds.

Ideally, reveal ties should not be used for more than half the total number of ties in a scaffold. Where this cannot be avoided, where they are likely to be removed for temporary access or for any other purpose or where it is not possible to provide any through or anchor ties (see page 33), the scaffold should be purpose designed.

RAKERS

Where it is not possible to provide normal ties, the stability of a scaffold can be achieved by the use of rakers. A single, unjointed raking tube not more than 6.4 m in length may be coupled at the top to the ledger at the second lift, extending at an angle not greater than 75° to the horizontal (4:1). The foot of the raking tube must be well founded and must always be tied back to the main scaffold. This arrangement can be used in place of a single tie.

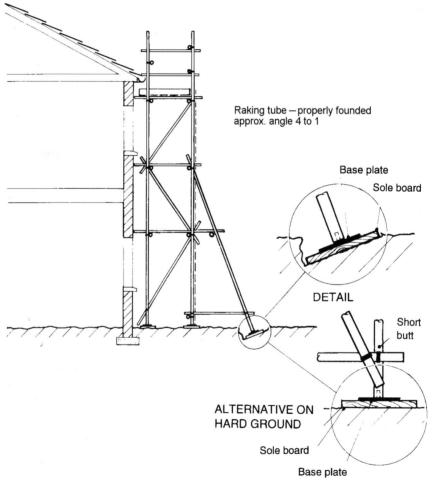

Raking tube — properly founded approx. angle 4 to 1

Base plate
Sole board

DETAIL

Short butt

ALTERNATIVE ON HARD GROUND

Sole board

Base plate

Fig. 5.6
(ladders omitted for clarity

First working lift

There may be occasions when a building that is under construction has as yet no firm parts on which to attach a tie. In such cases, when a working lift is required at 1.35 m (as in a putlog scaffold) or at 2 m (as in an independent scaffold), the scaffold may be stabilised temporarily by use of rakers. When only two ties are required (as in the case of a small house scaffold without returns), the rakers should be located one at either end. Rakers may also be used when a scaffold is being dismantled if it is not possible to stabilise the structure in any other way.

TIES

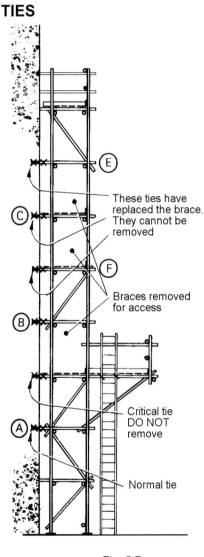

These ties have replaced the brace. They cannot be removed

Braces removed for access

Critical tie DO NOT remove

Normal tie

Fig. 5.7

Ties are essential to a scaffold's stability. As stated at the beginning of this chapter, the criteria governing the number and position of ties distinguish between scaffolds where a tie is likely to be removed and scaffolds with non-movable ties – and between sheeted and non-sheeted scaffolds. It should be emphasised, however, that no tie should be removed until a competent person has ensured there are sufficient alternative ties in place to prevent any reduction in the scaffold's stability.

A **critical tie** is a tie which has been placed in a scaffold:

- where ledger-to-ledger braces have been removed

- where a protective fan is erected

- where a cantilevered ladder stage, loading or landing stage is erected

- in the centre of a bridged scaffold.

Fig. 5.7 shows some examples of these. The scaffold was originally erected with normal ties at points A, B and C. The cantilevered ladder access must include a critical tie. Where the diagonal braces have been removed, on the fourth, sixth and seventh levels, additional ties must be added at points E and F. However, because braces are removed from two consecutive lifts (numbers 6 and 7), the normal tie at point C will also be a critical tie.

Remember, ordinary ties can be repositioned. Critical ties must not be removed.

REMOVING AND REPLACING TIES

When a scaffold is being designed or built, consideration needs to be given to access requirements or to the movement of materials, which may involve removing and replacing ties.

The finishing and other specialist trades will probably need to gain access to parts of the building that are obstructed by ties. It is essential to establish working procedures that are understood by all – this will avoid the danger posed by non-scaffolders taking matters into their own hands and removing and replacing ties.

Scaffold ties should only be removed and replaced under the supervision of an experienced and competent scaffolder, who will be aware of the dangers and who will be capable of making alternative arrangements to safeguard the stability of the structure.

Many serious accidents have been caused by the unauthorised removal or incorrect replacement of ties – accidents that could have been avoided by adequate supervision and the introduction of safe working practices.

SCAFFOLD TIES: Checklist

1. **Can the scaffold move away or towards the building?**

    If the answer is YES, the scaffold is not secure.

2. **Are all the ties fixed with load-bearing couplers?**

    All ties should be fixed with right-angle couplers. However, ties placed at a different angle may be fixed with swivel couplers.

3. **Are all the ties positioned correctly?**

    The best ties are connected to two standards, and are preferably braced.

    If the ties are connected to ledgers, the connection is best made within 300 mm of the standards.

4. **Is there a sufficient number of ties?**

    In the absence of expert advice that suggests larger spacing requirements, ties should be fixed on alternate lifts to the full height of the scaffold and at every other standard along its entire length.

    Reveal ties should not exceed 50% of the total number of ties.

5. **Are all the critical ties intact and secure?**

   Remember, critical ties are essential at any cantilevered point (fans, loading bays) and where braces have been removed for access.

   Remember also, never allow the removal of critical ties without expert advice from a competent scaffolder.

6. **Have any alterations been made to the scaffold?**

   Check items 1, 2, 3, 4 and 5 very carefully at the points where alterations have been made.

7. **Ensure the reveal ties have been physically checked and tightened.**

8. **Ensure all the anchorage points for screw or anchor ties are strong enough!**

9. **Always double-check the ties after adverse weather (especially high winds).**

10. **If in doubt, seek advice from the experts.**

6. WORKING PLATFORMS

A working platform can be anything from a minimum 600 mm-wide platform on a small putlog scaffold to a cantilevered structure, 60 m up near the top of a multistorey building.

The Work at Height Regulations 2005 require that, where work cannot be safely done on or from the ground or from part of the building or other permanent structure, there shall be provided, placed and kept in position for use and properly maintained either scaffolds or other means of support, all of which shall be sufficient and suitable for the purpose. The provision of a scaffold and working platform(s) is the most common method of meeting this requirement.

Other requirements relating to working platforms are that platforms must be 'close boarded' (that is, there should be no gaps through which persons or materials could fall); must be fitted with guard-rails and toe-boards; must be provided with some means of safe access (such as ladders and gangways); and that precautions should be taken to prevent tools, materials or equipment falling off, thus endangering those below. These requirements are illustrated in Fig. 6.1.

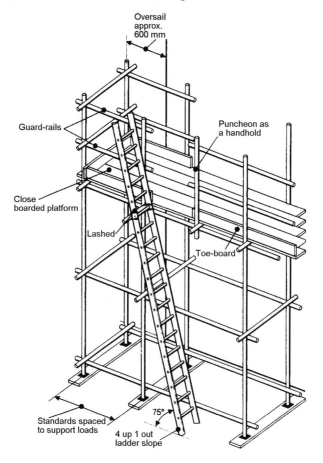

Fig. 6.1

Boarded lifts

The spacing of putlogs and transoms used to support a boarded platform is determined by the strength and thickness of the boards used. For 38 mm boards, this must not exceed 1.2 m and, for 50 m boards, this must not exceed 2.6 m. In practice, a standard 38 mm board (3.9 m long and allowing for the overhang and tolerance on the spacing of transoms) must be supported at four places.

Boards less than 2.7 m long should be supported on three transoms, and boards less than 2.13 m long should not be used unless they are physically tied or lashed down.

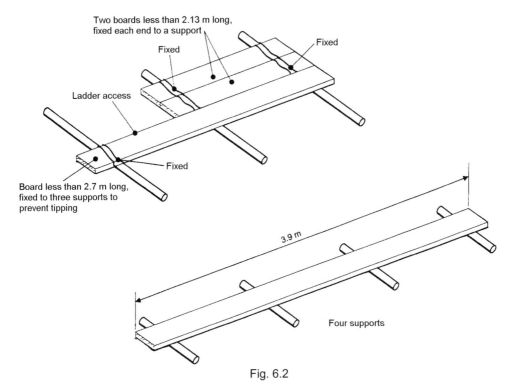

Fig. 6.2

The space between the edge of the working platform and the building must be as small as possible.

Boards must rest firmly and evenly on their supports. They should overhang the end transoms (their support) by **not less** than 50 mm and by **not more** than 150 mm in the case of 38 mm boards (approximately four times the board thickness), or 200 mm for 50 mm boards, unless they have been secured against tipping. Short boards will tip more easily than those of a full length and, to be safe, short boards (often taken to mean those less than 2.13 m long) should therefore be fixed at both ends.

The platform, wherever possible, should extend at least 600 mm beyond the end of any wall or working face. This distance is known as the oversail (see Fig. 6.1 on page 40).

Tripping hazards can be minimised by fitting bevelled pieces, or fillets, where boards overlap. As a general rule, boards should be laid with their ends butted.

Platform width

As previously stated, the *width* of the working platform will be determined by the platform's intended use.

Minimum width of 600 mm – this is considered adequate for access, inspection, gangways and runs.

Three boards wide – for operatives without materials, or for the passage of materials only. Fig. 6.3 shows a three-boarded platform being used by a painter. Normally, scaffolds are erected so that they do not foul such things as pipes, gutters and sills. An *inside board* can be fitted to extend the effective width of the platform and to reduce the gap between the platform and the building.

Four boards wide – this generally gives adequate space for operatives and materials and is often erected as a multi-trade platform, although there should always be a clear passage of 430 mm around or between materials to allow for movement. An inside board may be added for the same reasons as before.

Five boards wide – a five-board platform is commonly used by bricklayers. It is wide enough to permit materials to be stacked on the platform yet leaves enough room for the passage of operatives and materials and for operatives to work.

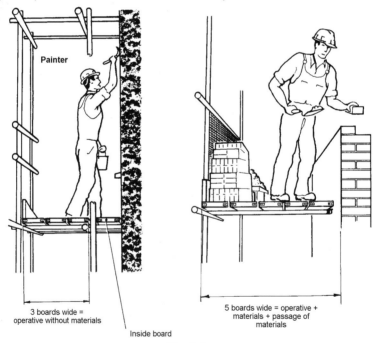

Painter

3 boards wide =
operative without materials

Inside board

5 boards wide = operative +
materials + passage of
materials

Fig. 6.3
(braces and fittings have been omitted for clarity)

Six to eight boards wide – these platforms are used by stonemasons and others to dress or shape stone or to undertake other heavy work, or to support a higher platform. These wider platforms are outside the scope of this book; they should only be erected under the supervision of a qualified scaffold design engineer.

Guard-rails and toe-boards

Every working platform (and scaffold) – no matter how small – that poses the risk of a fall that is likely to result in personal injury must be provided with guard-rails and toe-boards or barriers, unless other suitable and sufficient measures are taken to prevent persons from falling. Guard-rails, toe-boards and barriers may be removed for the length of time and to the extent necessary to gain access or egress for the performance of some particular work or task. However, while they are removed, the work or task shall not take place unless suitable and sufficient alternative safety measures are in place. The guard-rails, toe-boards and barriers must be replaced as soon as possible.

An example of a 'suitable alternative measure' would be the use of a restraint harness that prevents a worker from getting too close to an unprotected edge while moving materials that have been landed on a working platform.

Falling objects

Employers must take all reasonable steps to prevent scaffold materials (and other materials) from falling off a scaffold while it is being built, altered or dismantled. Scaffold fittings and tubes must not be thrown down from a height where they would be likely to cause injury. Where materials are likely to be stacked above the height of the toe-boards (a stack of bricks, for example), brick guards or other, similar barriers must be erected to prevent the materials falling off.

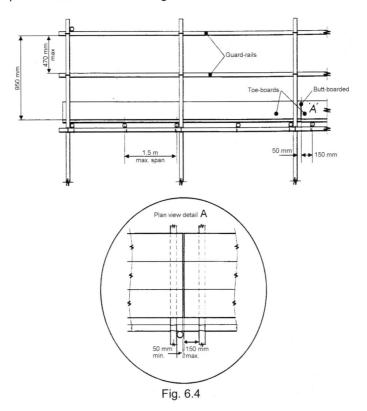

Fig. 6.4

Danger areas

While a scaffold is being built, altered or dismantled, and there is a risk of anyone falling or of anyone being struck by falling materials, then the area below/around the scaffold should be 'barriered off' to prevent unauthorised persons, especially members of the public and children, from getting too close. Suitable safety signs should also be put up.

Access

While a scaffold is being built, altered or dismantled, or at any other time when it is not available for use, safety signs must be put up and barriers used to prevent any unauthorised access to the scaffold. It is best if ladders are removed completely rather than merely a scaffolding board being lashed over the rungs. This is particularly the case in locations that are near such buildings as schools.

Access to a working platform is usually by ladder. This must be secured near the top and must extend above the level of the platform by a sufficient distance to allow for an adequate handhold (usually a distance of 1 m or five rungs, unless other adequate handholds are provided). If a ladder or a run of ladders rises more than 9 m, then safe landing platforms or rest areas must be provided at suitable intervals.

Care must be taken to see that there is adequate space between the rungs to give a firm foothold, and that there is no possibility of a person's foot being trapped between a rung and a ledger, transom or brace tube.

The landing area must be kept clear of such things as stacked materials, and be provided with guard-rails and toe-boards. The access should be as small as practicable. A removable hatch or partial barrier may be used to protect the access hole in the working platform.

When the platform is not in use, access must be blocked off to prevent unauthorised persons from climbing on to the platform and thus placing their lives in jeopardy. If there is a ladder access, the ladder should be removed, if possible (ladders are discussed in more detail in Chapter 7.

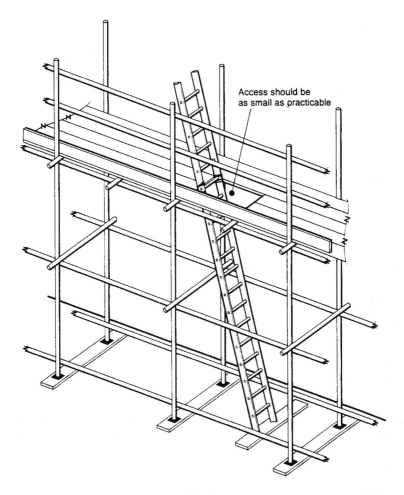

Access should be
as small as practicable

Fig. 6.5

Gangways and runs

Gangways and runs should be at least 600 mm wide if used only for access, and at least three boards wide if used for barrowing materials. Gangways and runs should be set level if possible, but may slope up to 1:4. If the slope is more than this, stepping laths must be provided which may incorporate a gap (not more than 100 mm wide for the barrow wheel).

Like all other platforms, where people could fall and injure themselves, gangways and runs must be provided with guard-rails and toe-boards.

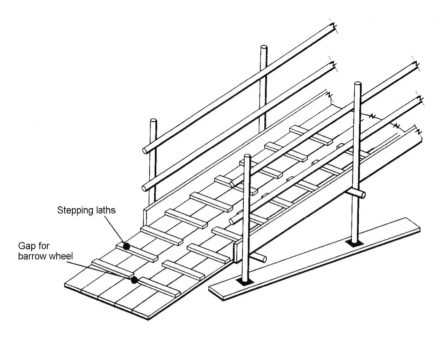

Stepping laths

Gap for
barrow wheel

Fig. 6.6

Keeping the platform clear

One of the greatest dangers associated with working platforms is that caused by obstructions to free access and movement. Working platforms must be kept free from unnecessary obstructions that can cause tripping and falling incidents.

Materials should not be stored on the working platform unless required for immediate use. They should be evenly distributed over the entire length of the platform, and care must be taken to stack heavy items as near to the standards as possible. Rubbish must be removed regularly and such things as trailing cables and ropes clipped up out of the way. The load on the platform must never exceed the design limits (see Table 2.1 on page 14).

7. LADDERS

Main types of ladder

Three main types of ladder are in use throughout the construction industry: standing ladders, pole ladders and extension ladders.

Standing timber ladders – these are single-section ladders of up to 7 m. The stiles are rectangular and the rungs may be rectangular or round.

Pole ladder – single-section ladders with the stiles made from a single pole cut lengthways, or halves of different poles of the same species of timber suitably matched. The advantage of this construction lies in the strength and flexibility gained by sectioning a pole lengthways. Pole ladders may be tapered or parallel. They are available in lengths up to 10 m.

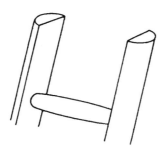

Fig. 7.1
(pole ladder)

Extension ladders – these comprise two or sometimes three sections coupled together, which extend by sliding over or inside each other. With a three-section ladder, lengths in excess of 30 m can be achieved. However, these are very seldom used in scaffolding work.

Aluminium ladders – most types of ladder are available in aluminium. They are lighter to carry than timber ladders, are strong and will not warp.

Overhead electrical cables

Ladders, including wooden ladders, should not be used close to overhead electric cables or other electrical supply equipment due to the risk of an electric shock. Even though a wooden ladder may appear to be 'safe', such things as metal in the ladder, dampness, varnish and dirt can cause the ladder to conduct electricity.

Condition of ladders

Regulations require that ladders must be in good repair and strong enough for the job. They should be checked for damage, faults and wear before use. Ladders should not be painted or treated in such a way as to conceal defects. New ladders can be protected by a transparent coating, such as a varnish, shellac or clear preservative.

Because ladders are 'work equipment', they should be inspected by a competent person on a regular basis.

Inspection of ladders

Stiles – check stiles for warping, splintering, cracking and bruising (which admits moisture into the timber and encourages decay). The feet of the stiles are particularly vulnerable to damage.

Rungs – rungs should not be worn or missing. Examine rungs especially at the point where they enter the stiles. If they are wedged, these should be correctly positioned. Grasp the rungs firmly and twist them to make sure none rotate.

Soundness of construction – take each end of the ladder in turn and try to pull the stiles apart – then push them together. Movement will indicate a defective ladder. A further check should be made by laying the ladder flat, raising one end and attempting to push one stile while pulling the other. If the stiles can be removed relative to each other in this way, the rungs are loose. *Check that metal tie rods are in place and secure and that none are missing.*

Damaged or worn ladders

Defective ladders must be taken out of service as soon as the fault or damage is discovered. They should be marked clearly 'DEFECTIVE – DO NOT USE' and remain out of use until repaired. Where it is not possible or practical to repair a ladder that is unfit for use, it should be destroyed immediately.

Fig. 7.2

Carrying ladders

Short ladders can be carried by one person either vertically against the shoulder or horizontally across the shoulder, as shown in Fig. 7.2.

Long ladders should be carried horizontally on the shoulders by two people, one either end, holding the upper stile, as shown in Fig. 7.3, in a comfortable manner.

When carrying a ladder, care should be taken in rounding corners or passing between or under obstacles. The risk assessment should state that ladders are never carried in an upright position near overhead electric power lines. If a premises has an overhead mains electricity supply (these are usually found in older premises in rural locations), then the scaffold's design and the use of ladders will need to take this into account.

Fig. 7.3

Erecting and lowering ladders

To erect a ladder, first lay it flat on the ground with the foot towards the base of the structure it is to be set against. One person should stand at the bottom of the ladder with one foot braced it against it to prevent movement. The second person should go to the head of the ladder and, taking hold of the top rung, raise it over their head. Grasping the ladder rung by rung, they should move towards the bottom of the ladder, raising it as they go. The anchor person grasps the stiles as they come within reach and helps to draw the ladder into the upright position.

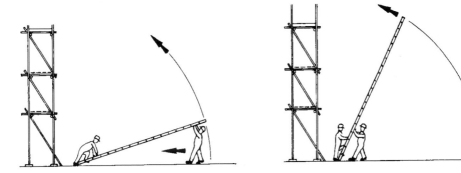

Fig. 7.4

This sequence is reversed when lowering a ladder.

One person can raise a short ladder by placing the foot of the ladder against a wall or fixture and pushing it upright from the head.

Placing ladders

The angle at which a ladder is set up against a structure should be 75° or a ratio of 4 up to 1 out. The base of the ladder should rest on firm, even ground. Never pack one side of the ladder to compensate for uneven ground; either level the ground or bury the foot of the ladder so that it stands evenly. On soft earth, put a board down and tamp it into the earth. However, suitable precautions must be taken so that the ladder's stiles do not slip on the board.

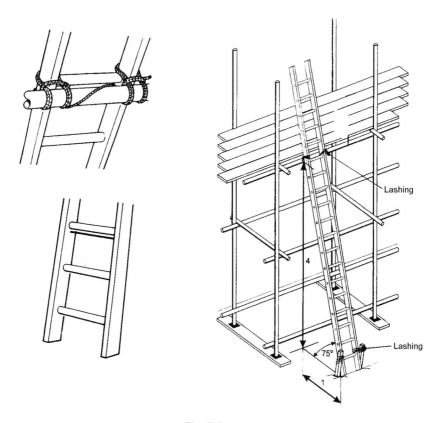

Fig. 7.5

The essential point is that the ladder's foot should rest on a secure, stable base. Never attempt to gain extra height by placing the ladder on boxes, drums or any other type of makeshift platform. If it is not long enough for the job, get a longer one!

Ladders must be secured and must extend above the level of the platform by a sufficient distance to allow for an adequate handhold while getting on to the working platform (usually a distance of 1 m or five rungs, unless other adequate handholds are provided). If a ladder or a run of ladders rises more than 9 m, then safe landing platforms or rest areas must be provided at suitable intervals.

The landing rung should be level with, or slightly above, the working platform. There should be space above each rung for a proper foothold. Ensure the foot cannot become trapped between rungs and by obstructions behind the ladder.

Where ladders are positioned on intermediate platforms, these should be close boarded and provided with toe-boards and guard-rails.

When moving or placing ladders, beware of overhead power lines and other electrical hazards.

Lashings and ties

A ladder must be supported and held by the stiles, never by the rungs. It should be held securely in position so that it cannot move from its top or bottom points.

Ladders provided for scaffolding access should be securely lashed from stiles to the scaffold (ledger or extended transoms), using a square lashing as shown in Fig. 7.5, at or just below the upper landing. Proprietary fixings (i.e. ladder ties and clamps) may be used, but care should be taken to use the correct type. Some require the stile cross-section to be rectangular and are thus not suitable for use with pole ladders.

Ladder clamp

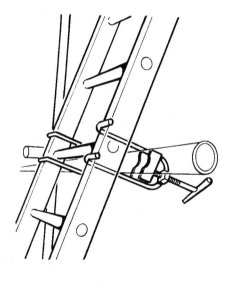

Fig. 7.6

Long ladders may require a lashing or tie at the mid-point to prevent excessive movement. In some circumstances the use of ladder stays will make a job both easier and safer.

The ladder must not rest against or be lashed to plastic fascias, gutters, drainpipes or any other fittings or fragile surfaces. Bracing boards should be used for windows and other openings.

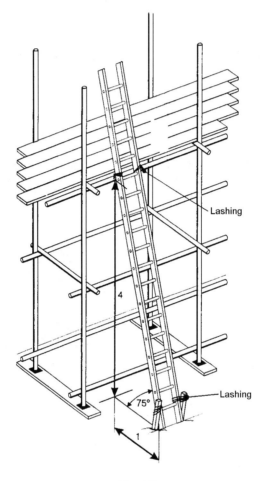

Fig. 7.7

Use of ladders

Ladders should always be used in such a way that a secure handhold and secure support are always available to the user, and so that the user can maintain a safe handhold while carrying objects. Tools may be carried up in pockets, on a belt designed for the purpose or in a shoulder bag. The carrying of excessive weights must be avoided. If a hoist line is available, it should be used. Whichever method is used, it should leave both hands free to hold on to the ladder.

A secure footing is essential in any ladder work, and this requires sound footwear, with the soles in good condition and free of mud or grease. In wet or icy weather, extra care will be necessary to maintain a secure footing.

Check there is no one else on the ladder before ascending or descending it. Always face the ladder and hold on to the stiles, not the rungs. The thighs and hips should be kept between the stiles, and the feet should be placed in the middle of the rungs – ladders are not designed for any degree of side loading. Do not climb higher than the third rung from the top.

Overreaching or stretching while on a ladder is extremely dangerous and can lead to loss of balance. If the work area cannot be reached, move the ladder or obtain a longer one, as appropriate.

Preventing unauthorised access

While a scaffold is not available for use (including during its erection, when it is being altered or dismantled and outside working hours), unauthorised access must be prevented. This is best done by the removal of any ladder access rather than by lashing a scaffold board across the rungs. Warning notices must also be placed on the scaffold, and suitable barriers should be erected to prevent access.

Fig. 7.8

Care and storage of ladders and steps

Ladders, especially those made of wood, should not be stored outside for long periods where the weather can damage them. They are best stored inside, but if this is not possible they should be covered or stored in a protected position.

Ladders should either be hung horizontally on a rack, supported under the stiles, or rested on blocks, again under the stiles. They must not be supported by the rungs (this can loosen or otherwise damage them) or stored flat on the ground or against walls, radiators or hot pipes which can lead to warping, sagging and distortion. Deposits of mud or grease should be cleaned off the rungs and cement wiped away before it hardens (aluminium ladders may be corroded by wet lime or cement). Pulleys and hinges need lubrication, and cords and ropes should be checked.

Any damage or deterioration should be reported to the person responsible for the equipment.

8. MANUAL LIFTING AND HANDLING

The erection and dismantling of scaffolds involve a large amount of manual handling. Assessments carried out under the Manual Handling Operations Regulations should be used to establish safe working practices as regards manual handling, and any training or further training that employees may need.

Weights of materials

Steel scaffold tubes
4.4 kg per metre
28.2 kg for a 6.4 m tube
36 tubes = 1 metric tonne

Fittings, singles
0.6 – 1 kg each (0.8 kg average)
1,250 = I metric tonne

Fittings, doubles
1.2 – 1.6 kg each (1.4 kg average)
440 = 1 metric tonne

Boards 38 mm
6 kg per metre
23.4 kg for a 3.9 m board
43 = 1 metric tonne

Boards 50 mm
8 kg per metre

Boards 63 mm
10 kg per metre

Pole ladders
4.3 kg per metre

Of all the serious accidents in the building and construction industry each year 30% involve injuries sustained through manual lifting and the handling of materials and equipment. A further 30% are caused by slips, trips and falls.

Scaffolders spends most of their time lifting and handling scaffolding material under a variety of conditions. The nature of the job dictates that they must be mentally alert to the dangers inherent in a physically strenuous job. Muscles and joints can be strained by sudden and awkward movements – twisting or jerking while lifting or carrying a load, or by attempting to lift too heavy a load. Back injuries are common. These may be the cumulative effect of repeated minor injuries or the result of abrupt strain.

The risk of injury can be reduced by adopting a mental attitude that encourages good lifting techniques. Stoop lifting should be avoided because it greatly increases the chance of back injury. The stress imposed on a rounded back is much greater than if the trunk is kept upright, using the leg and thigh muscles to power the lift.

Fig. 8.1 is an example of stoop lifting. The trunk is twisted to enable the hand to reach down to the load, which is grasped by the fingertips, and the knees have been locked to prevent the man overbalancing. The muscles in the lower back are about to do the work and will come under great strain as the worker attempts simultaneously to straighten up and lift the load. The consequence of this may be a slipped disc or torn back muscles.

THIS DIAGRAM DEPICTS

DANGEROUS PRACTICE

Fig. 8.1

Kinetic lifting

The kinetic method of lifting enables the worker to make full use of the body's own weight and momentum to initiate the lift. The natural shape of the spine is maintained throughout (although the body may be bent forward the spine should remain straight) and the lift is powered by the strong leg and thigh muscles. This method of lifting involves the minimum amount of muscular effort and reduces stress and fatigue.

The following six key factors should be practised until they become second nature – a single, co-ordinated action.

1. **Feet** Any lifting or handling can only be successful if it is carried out on a firm base. The scaffolder may work from the ground or on a temporary platform, and it is essential that the feet are placed so that a good balance is maintained throughout the lift.

   There is no correct or exact distance apart for the feet. Each individual has to consider their own weight, height and build. In general terms the feet should be in line with the lift, comfortably apart, with one foot slightly in front of the other. The rear foot should point forward when lifting, in the direction of movement. This position gives a good, adaptable balance and a wide enough base to perform the lift.

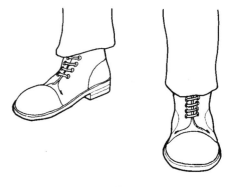

Fig. 8.2

2. **Legs** Having established a good base for the lift and realised that it may be necessary to make adjustments of balance, it naturally follows that the legs must be relaxed sufficiently to achieve flexibility. To obtain flexibility, both knees must be unlocked to allow the feet to adjust automatically. This is a requirement for all good movement.

    While it is important to unlock and bend the knees, they should not be placed into the complete squat position, as this will place extreme pressure on the knee joints. Fig. 8.3 shows the forward leg at a 90° angle while the back leg will provide the thrust for the lift. Although the lifter is only using one hand, the weight will be taken through the centre line of the body, thus maximising the use of body weight.

Fig. 8.3

3. **Head** The head should be gently raised and the chin tucked firmly in. This will not only straighten the neck but also the whole spine, and it will bring about many other corrections in body movement, automatically lifting the chest and preparing the arms for a more efficient action. This head action should be carried out at the initial stage of all lifting movements.

4. **Straight back** A bent back is a weak back. It will lead to excessive muscular tension and damage to the spine. It will also undermine shoulder and arm efficiency. Generally, if the correct head position is adopted, then the back can be kept straight, even if it is not vertical.

    The back should straighten automatically, prior to the hands taking the load. Fig. 8.4 shows a difficult lift: the feet are well planted, the knees well positioned and the back straightened as the chin is being drawn in.

Fig. 8.4

5. **Arms** The arms should be as close to the body as possible. The further they are extended the greater the strain. The elbows should be kept into the body.

Fig. 8.5

6. **Grip** A good hand grip is essential. Scaffolders spend the majority of their time handling tube, which, because of its shape, is difficult to grasp.

    Whenever possible, one hand should be below the load, with most of the weight being taken by the palm and roots of the fingers.

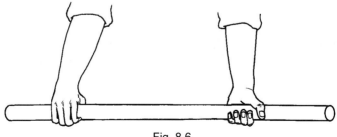

Fig. 8.6

58

Sequence of lifting a scaffold tube

Before lifting any weight, a worker must ensure that the ground area is clear and free from tripping hazards. It is important to see that no-one is in the way and that there is nothing likely to obstruct the lift. The weight should be within the lifting capacity of the individual worker. The load should be approached squarely, facing in the direction of travel. The feet must be placed apart with one foot slightly in front of the other to maintain a comfortable balance, the knees bent and the body as close to the load as possible.

The tube should be grasped firmly, with the arms kept as close in to the body as possible, grasping the tube in front of the body. Adjust the position of the head (head up – chin in) and begin to lift using the leg and thigh muscles. As the tube is raised transfer the grip to maintain a balanced grasp on the tube, holding it close to the body.

The weight of the body can be easily transferred from one foot to another, ensuring that the balance is maintained and enabling the load to be taken by the whole body.

This use of the bodyweight if best illustrated when the scaffolder is carrying long tubes in the vertical position. Fig. 8.7 shows the back leg still in the thrust position, and the front foot in the direction of the lift. The back is straight and the head erect.

The weight is taken on the palms of the hands and the entire bodyweight is positioned to resist any movement of the tube. Note that the top forefinger is extended along the tube and will act as a sensor to give early warning of any movement of the tube, enabling the feet to be repositioned to maintain a good balance.

Fig. 8.7

Remember!

Aches and pains are warning signals and indicate fatigue and stress. If ignored, the outcome may well be some form of injury as a result of incorrect lifting techniques.

LIFTING SCAFFOLD TUBES

The following sequences show some of the common handling and lifting tasks required of scaffolders every day.

Safety check

Before lifting, check that:

- the area is clear of any tripping hazards, including the route you are going to take and where you will land the tube

- your action will not endanger anybody

- you are capable of lifting the load.

Lifting a long tube

In Fig. 8.8, the correct foot position has been adopted – the front foot in the direction of the lift, and the rear foot ready to thrust behind the load. The chin is still to be tucked in, but the back is straight.

Fig. 8.8

Fig. 8.9

The tube is lifted – the feet have been adjusted to allow the lifter to walk to the centre of the tube using a hand-over-hand movement to maintain the weight of the load. The chin has been tucked in, thus maintaining a straight back.

Having reached the centre of the tube, the hands adjust for balance. The hand which is placed over the tube is bearing very little weight because the hand under the tube is positioned closer to the centre of the tube and is therefore taking most of the load.

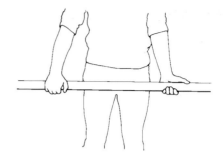

Fig. 8.10

Now the tube is ready to be raised to the carrying position which in this case, is on the shoulder.

As the lift is carried out it will be necessary for the body to be turned in the direction of the intended line of carry.

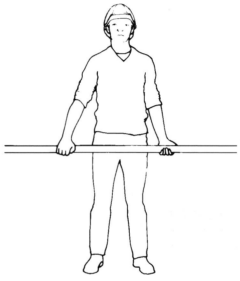

Fig. 8.11

The knees are unlocked and ready to allow the feet to adjust to the new position.

The arms and shoulders are used to begin the lift.

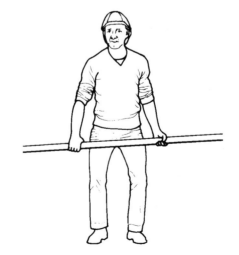

Fig. 8.12

As the lift nears the correct height the feet have begun the adjustment that will allow the body to turn under the tube and allow the shoulder to receive the weight.

Fig. 8.13

Fig. 8.14

The load has been released by the load-bearing hand and transferred to the shoulder, and the other hand is kept in position to steady the tube. The feet have nearly completed the adjustments.

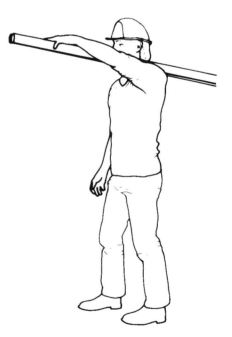

The shoulder hand has been placed into the steadying position and the feet have completed the adjustments, thus allowing the body to complete the turn safely.

The lift is complete, and the carry can begin.

To place the tube back on the ground, the actions are reversed.

Fig. 8.15

LONG TUBE (vertical carry)

Again before performing the lift, ensure:

- the area is clear of tripping hazards, including the route you are going to take and where you will land the tube

- your lift action will not endanger anyone

- you are capable of handling the load.

As you are about to carry the tube in the vertical position, ensure:

- the area and space above head height are clear along the entire length of the carry

- there are no overhead cables in the vicinity.

The same actions as in the previous lift are carried out until the load is taken in the centre by the hands. The end of the tube should be butted against something solid. If nothing is available, another worker can use the instep of their boot to 'block' the end of the tube.

Fig. 8.16

Note: **Never** use the toe of the boot because the tube could twist out on either side and cause a very painful injury.

Fig. 8.17

Having butted the tube, it can be raised above the head and, with the bodyweight behind the tube and the palms and heels of the hands bearing the weight, the tube can be walked to a near upright position.

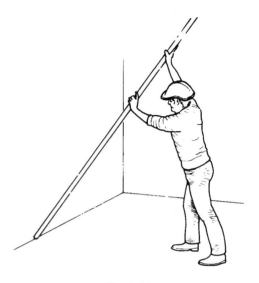

Fig. 8.18

The tube is now ready to be lifted. With the knees unlocked, the back straight and the chin tucked in, the bodyweight is in a position to resist the movement of the tube.

Note: The high-hand forefinger is again acting as a sensor.

Fig. 8.19

Fig. 8.20

To begin the lift, the knees bend and the hands maintain the same distance apart when sliding down the tube. This will incline the tube even more towards the lifter, who accommodates the movement by bending the high arm slightly. It is this arm that is about to take the entire load – the bottom hand is only acting as a guide and restraint.

The lift is completed as the legs straighten.

The legs must remain unlocked to allow the feet to make the necessary adjustments that will permit the body to change to the direction of carry.

Fig. 8.21

With the manoeuvre completed the carry can begin.

Note: The bottom hand is placed round the **outside** of the tube to act as a restraint, while the top hand bears the full weight of the tube.

Fig. 8.22

Lifting short tubes

This method is normally used when lifting short tubes (between 1.5 m and 2.4 m) that are placed at ground level.

The natural position is adopted for the selection of the tube.

Because the initial selection is made by inserting the fingers into the ends of the tubes, it is essential to ensure the tubes are free of sharp edges, and so it is advisable that suitable gloves are worn.

Fig. 8.23

As soon as they are clear of the ground, the free hand is placed under the tubes to assist in control.

Note: Three tubes have been raised, although the third one is hidden by the other two.

Fig. 8.24

The tubes are now upright and can be adjusted to form a pyramid pattern with the base towards the shoulder.

The knees have remained unlocked and the back is still straight. The feet have made the necessary adjustments. The chin remains firmly tucked in. The bodyweight is still behind the load.

Fig. 8.25

Both the top and bottom hands slide down the tubes as the knees bend. This will allow the shoulder to be positioned just below the centre of the tubes.

The weight is taken on the shoulder with the forward hand and shoulder arm acting as a restraint.

Note: The rear foot is in the thrust position and the bodyweight is positioned behind the load.

As the shoulder is below the centre point of the load, the load will easily tip over into the horizontal position, with the front hand steadying the momentum.

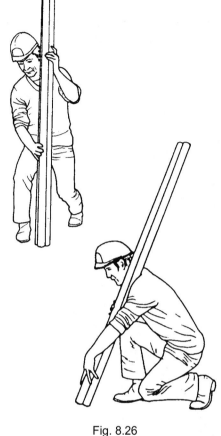

Fig. 8.26

Fig. 8.27

As the tubes reach the horizontal position, the legs carry out and complete the lift.

With the lift completed, the carry can begin.

Fig. 8.28

To place the tubes back on the ground the movements are repeated in reverse.

The figures have shown a scaffolder lifting tubes at ground level. It can be seen clearly that this job is physically strenuous. Scaffold tubes are somewhat unwieldy and difficult to handle, which is one of the reasons why mechanical handling should be used whenever possible. This problem is made even more difficult when tubes are handled vertically.

The scaffolder has to use the same handling skills when working on a three or four-board-wide platform that is at a considerable height above the ground. Apart from using the correct techniques, a scaffolder must be even more careful when making the usual pre-lift checks before handling long tubes vertically.

Fig. 8.29 show some of the dangers that may be encountered.

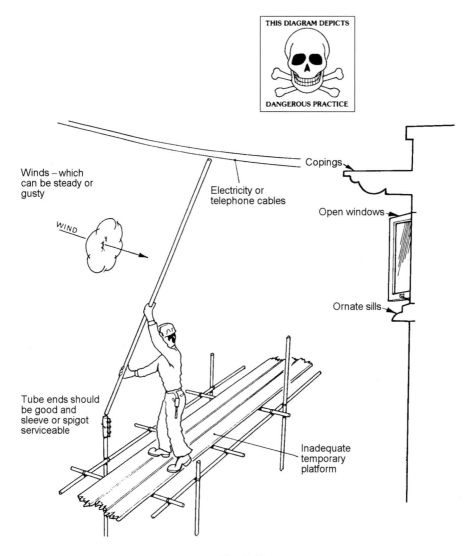

Fig. 8.29

9. ROPES, KNOTS and HITCHES

The correct use of rope and knots is very important in scaffolding work. Ropes are used for raising and lowering tubes, boards and fittings, and for lashing ladders and boards (although wire lashing is sometimes used).

Types of rope

Ropes can be classified broadly as those made of natural and those made of synthetic fibres.

Natural fibre	Synthetic fibre
Manila	Nylon (Polyamide)
Sisal	Polyester
Hemp	Polyethylene
Cotton	Polypropylene
Coir	

Ropes greater than 8 mm in diameter are generally supplied in 220 m lengths. The most common size of rope used for lifting materials in scaffolding is 18 mm in diameter. This is the correct size for use with a gin wheel. Smaller wire ropes are used for lashing ladders.

Ropes are also classified by the number of strands and the manner in which the strands are twisted and plaited together. One type in common use is the three-strand plain (or hawser-laid) rope.

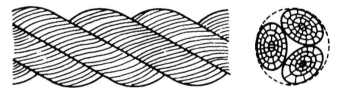

Fig. 9.1

Synthetic-fibre ropes are replacing natural-fibre ropes. The reasons for this are that they are stronger, less liable to chemical attack, completely resistant to mildew and rot and have better water resistance. However, they do burn more easily than natural fibre and care should be taken to avoid excessive friction in sheaves and blocks. It is also important to make sure that the correct size of rope is used in a block.

Care must also be taken when oxyacetylene cutters or blowlamps are in use. The flame must not be allowed to come into contact with any synthetic or natural-fibre rope.

Perhaps the most suitable ropes for use in scaffolding are of staple-spun or fibre-film polypropylene. These are not as strong as nylon and polyester but are considerably cheaper. They are light, durable and cheaper than manila, are particularly water resistant and float in water. The only drawback to this type of material is that, as the temperature increases, it becomes softer and loses strength. However, this only becomes significant above 50°C where there is a loss of 13% in strength.

Care and use of fibre ropes

Fibre rope, like wire rope, can be damaged while it is being removed from the shipping coil. A new coil or rope should be laid flat on the floor and unwound through the coil in a counter-clockwise direction. Even when the rope is unwound correctly, loops and kinks may form and these must be carefully removed to avoid damaging the rope.

After use, the rope should be re-coiled in a clockwise direction. When coiling the rope, remove kinks as they form.

Storage

Poor storage can cause fibre rope to deteriorate as rapidly as can harsh use. To keep ropes in good condition for as long as possible:

- Store them in a dry cool place that has good air circulation.

- Do not store ropes on the floor, in boxes, or in cupboards where air circulation is restricted. They should be hung up in loose coils on large-diameter wooden pegs well above the floor.

- Protect ropes from wet weather and sunlight. They should be kept away from boilers, radiators, steam pipes and other sources of heat and all exhaust gases.

- Dry and clean wet ropes before storing them. Moisture not only hastens decay but also causes the rope to kink very easily. If a wet rope becomes frozen, it must not be disturbed until it is completely thawed, otherwise the frozen fibres will break when handled. Allow wet and frozen rope to dry naturally. Too much heat will cause the fibres to become brittle and the rope will be unfit for further service.

Use of ropes

- Never overload a rope or exceed its safe working load (SWL).

- Never drag a rope along the ground. The outside will be damaged and grit will become embedded and destroy the internal fibres.

- Never drag a rope over sharp or rough edges and never drag one part of a rope over another.

- Avoid all but straight line pulls with rope; a knot or bend will weaken it by approximately 50%.

- Pack all sharp corners when lifting materials to prevent them abrading the rope.

- Never use fibre rope near welding or flame-cutting operations. The sparks and molten metal can damage the rope or set it on fire. Avoid exposure to all forms of heat.

- When a wire rope is attached to a hook or ring a thimble should be placed in the loop or eye to reduce the wear on the rope.

Inspection

The only way to determine the safety of a rope, and its load-carrying ability is by regularly inspecting every metre of its length. The main points to be watched for are external wear, cuts and abrasions, internal wear between the strands and deterioration of the fibres.

If the rope is dirty and in poor condition, if the strands have begun to unlay, or if the rope has lost its life and elasticity, it should not be used for lifting purposes. Should there be any doubt as to whether or not a rope is fit for use, it should be replaced at once. Never risk danger to life or damage to property by taking chances.

When a rope has been condemned, it should be destroyed at once or cut up into short lengths so that it cannot be used for lifting purposes.

KNOTS, BENDS AND HITCHES

Knots and bends reduce the strength of a rope by up to 50% and hitches reduce the strength by up to 25%. This relates to the final strength of the rope and **not** to the resistance of any given knot to slip.

Common knots

The most common knots and hitches used in scaffolding are as follows:

Rolling hitch
This is the preferred knot for lifting tubes and boards.

Figure-of-eight knot
Used to lock a rope in position (i.e. to prevent it sliding through a block or temporarily to prevent the end of the rope from fraying).

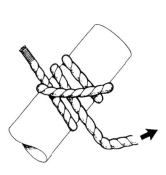

Fig. 9.2
(rolling hitch)

Fig. 9.3
(figure-of-eight knot)

Timber hitch

This is suitable for lifting boards. It is sometimes used in conjunction with a half-hitch.

Square lashing

Used in scaffolding to secure ladders to the scaffold structure. Begin the lashing with a clove hitch and pass the rope over and behind the transom or ledger and back in front of the ladder stile four times. Make two trapping turns and finish off with another clove hitch. Lash both stiles.

Fig. 9.4
(timber hitch)

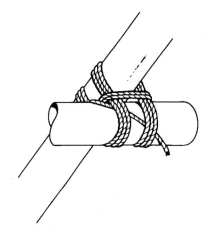
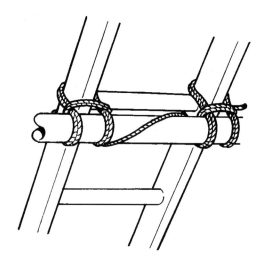

Fig. 9.5
(square lashing)

10. RAISING AND LOWERING MATERIALS

Mechanical handling should always be the preferred choice when raising or lowering scaffold materials. On occasions, however, this is not practicable and an alternative method has to be used.

A scaffold gang will spend a great deal of its time during the erection and dismantling of scaffolds raising or lowering tubes, boards and fittings. This work has to be carried out in all kinds of weather and at many different locations – in the high street or other public places, on enclosed building sites or on some major civil engineering construction in a remote area. The methods used to raise and lower scaffolding materials will be determined by the extent and type of the scaffold being built and the equipment available.

The methods available will generally fall into one or other of the following categories:

Handballing/chaining	Forklift truck	Gin wheel and rope
Light line/hand line	Goods hoist	Tower crane

This chapter examines these various methods and suggests how risks can be reduced and working efficiency improved.

Handballing, sometimes called 'chaining', is the method normally adopted on the first few lifts of a scaffold. The gang will form a chain up the face of the scaffold and pass tubes and boards from one to another. Fig. 10.1 shows a good example of handballing.

Note: If the work does not take place behind a double handrail, then suitable and sufficient alternative measures must be taken to prevent the risk of anyone falling.

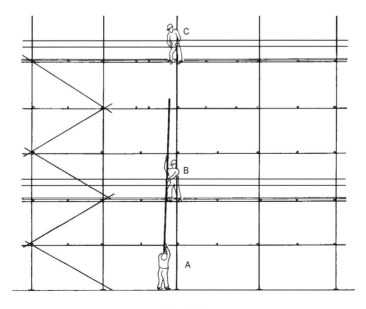

Fig. 10.1

Person A has passed a long tube to B who, like the person at C, has adopted a good safe position where they can use both hands to raise the tube. A should not release the tube until B has clearly indicated that they have full control of the tube. A good method of communication is for the person receiving the tube to call 'my tube' when they are ready and in control.

Light line, sometimes called a 'hand line', is often used on scaffolds up to 15 m high. Tubes, boards or sacks of fittings are tied to the lower end of a 13 mm fibre rope and then hauled up by hand. It is essential to adopt a safe position when doing this. This involves using a standard for support, one leg being placed behind the standard to act as an anchor and to prevent the lifter from overbalancing. Again, if not done from behind double handrails, then suitable and sufficient alternative measures must be taken to prevent the risk of falls.

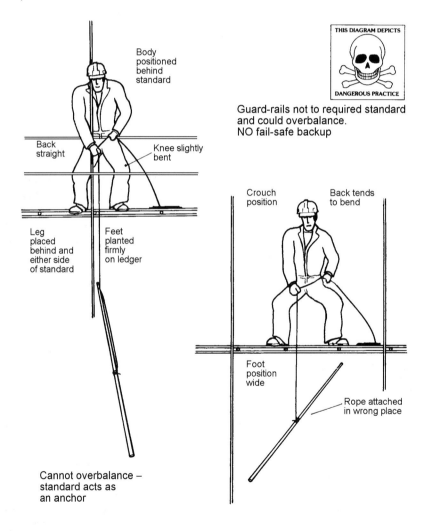

Fig. 10.2

The gin wheel and rope is commonly used to raise materials that are tied to the end of a 18 mm diameter rope passed over a single wheel pulley. The gin wheel (pulley) is fixed to a horizontal cantilevered tube. The material is then hauled up to the working level by the person on the ground.

Two types of gin wheel are available, the 'ring' type and the 'hook' type. The ring type is designed to fit over a scaffold tube. The hook type only differs at the point of suspension: instead of a ring, the pulley is suspended by a hook.

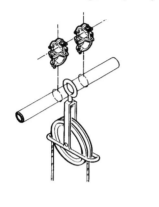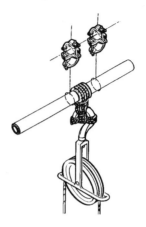

Fig. 10.3

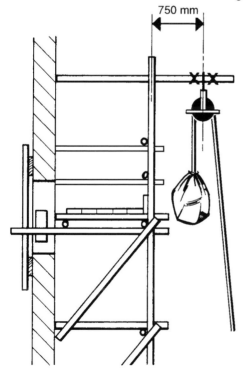

750 mm

Fig. 10.4

The gin wheel is usually suspended from a cantilevered tube. This should be fixed properly with right-angle couplers, preferably to two standards approximately 2 m above the landing place. If the cantilevered part of the tube is unsupported, the point of suspension should not extend more than 750 mm. Check fittings should be fixed either side of the suspension point to ensure the gin wheel cannot move. If a hook-type wheel is used, it must be suspended on a 6 mm wire lashing with at least five turns around the hook and tube, and the open end of the hook must be moused to ensure it cannot be displaced.

The fibre rope should have a minimum diameter of 18 mm and a stopper knot (usually a figure-of-eight knot) should be tied near the ends so that it cannot run through the gin wheel.

75

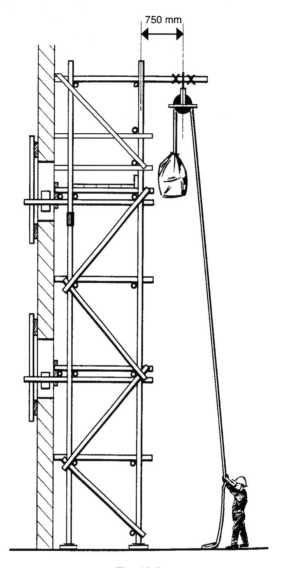

750 mm

Fig. 10.5

The recommended maximum load that should be raised or lowered by a gin wheel and rope at any one time is about 30 kg. However, it must also be within the capabilities of the employee who is pulling on the rope and subject to an assessment under the Manual Handling Operations Regulations.

Care should be taken, particularly when lowering materials. If the weight is too great, the person lowering will be unable to control the load, which then falls, or they may be pulled off their feet or the complete assembly may collapse. A proper assessment under the regulations will prevent this from occurring.

Fork-lift trucks are frequently used to raise and lower scaffold material to and from the scaffolding. It is essential that the fork-lift driver is competent and authorised to drive, and is made aware of the weight of the load. They should also know the load-bearing capacity of the scaffold. Working platforms are sometimes overloaded by enthusiastic operators who are not aware of these factors.

Where a fork-lift truck is used for loading a platform, a second front ledger is sometimes fitted, in front of and below the main front ledger to provide extra protection from impact and as a 'check fitting'.

Tower cranes are often used to raise and lower large loads of scaffolding material during the construction of multistorey blocks. The Lifting Operations and Lifting Equipment Regulations 1998 (LOLER) apply, which should ensure that all lifts are properly planned and carried out. The driver should be made aware of the weights involved, and it is essential to ensure that the scaffold is capable of bearing the load.

Extreme care should be taken by the person receiving the load. The crane driver has only limited control and so the receiver could be struck by the load.

Goods hoists should only be used to raise or lower material that can be safely contained within the area and the SWL of the hoist platform. This rule generally restricts the scaffolder to very short tubes (transoms) and scaffold fittings.

Remember, many accidents are caused by falling materials. Ensure that all material is raised, lowered and placed safely and securely on the platform.

11. ORGANISATION AND WORKING METHODS

Erecting a scaffold involves a great deal of hard physical effort – it is hard work and is generally only undertaken by fit young persons. The Work at Height Regulations require all work at height to be properly planned, appropriately supervised and carried out in a safe manner. As with much scaffolding work, there is no absolutely right or correct way of doing the job – much will depend on the particular circumstances: the height and extent of the structure; the nature and location of the site; the numbers employed; and so on. It remains true, however, that unless some thought is given to planning and preparing for the job, a great deal of time and effort can be wasted.

Wasted effort means unnecessary expense, tired operatives (who are likely to cut corners or make mistakes) and substandard work. The result may be an increased risk of accidents to all those using the scaffold and even to innocent passers-by.

Example 1A

A gang of scaffolders arrives at a site to erect an independent scaffold, 36 m long by 25 m high. They have a choice of unloading at points, A, B or C. They choose C, unload the lorry and begin laying out material from point A, working back towards the unloading point.

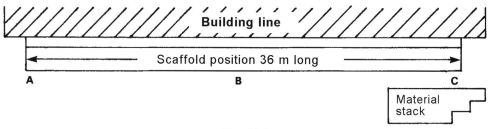

Fig. 11.1

The material has to be carried and laid out for each of the lifts.

Each 6 m section of the 36 m run contains:

    2 x 6.5 m ledgers
    2 x 2.5 m braces
    6 x 1.8 m transoms
    26 scaffold fittings

Each lift of scaffold requires one person to carry and lay out these materials six times.

The total distance walked is shown in Fig. 11.2:

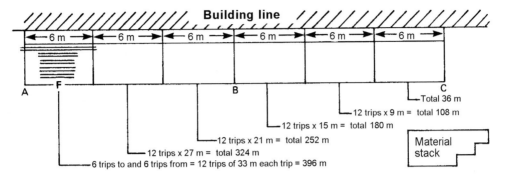

Fig. 11.2

Each trip comprises one carry and one return trip, so that each 6 m run requires:

12 trips of 33 m which equals 396 m   12 trips of 15 m which equals 180 m
12 trips of 27 m which equals 324 m   12 trips of 9 m which equals 108 m
12 trips of 21 m which equals 252 m   12 trips of 3 m which equals 36 m

This makes a total of 1,296 m per lift walked by one person. As there are 13 lifts to be laid out, one person must walk 16.848 km (13 x 1,296), which is the equivalent of 10½ miles.

Note: the above calculations do not include sway braces, boards, guard-rails, toe-boards, standards, ladders or ties.

Example 1B The material is unloaded at point B (Fig. 11.3).

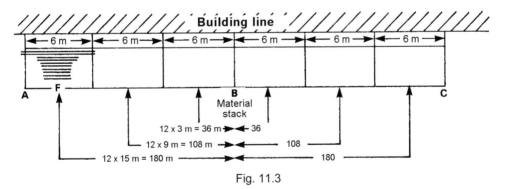

Fig. 11.3

Each 6 m section would require the same number of trips (i.e. 12) but, as the materials are distributed from the centre, each 36 m run will require:

12 trips of 15 m which equals 180 m   12 trips of 15 m which equals 180 m
12 trips of 9 m which equals 108 m   12 trips of 9 m which equals 108 m
12 trips of 3 m which equals 36 m   12 trips of 3 m which equals 36 m

This makes a total of 648 m per lift to be walked by one person. Again, 648 m multiplied by 13 lifts equals 8,424 m, which is nearly 8.5 km (or just over 5 miles).

Comparison

The distance between positions B and C is only 18 m but, through lack of foresight, over **10 tonnes** of material has been carried an additional 8 km. By thinking ahead and planning where the materials should be unloaded (and before that, at the depot, of how they should first be loaded onto the lorry), the effort, time and cost of laying out the materials can be considerably reduced, as can the risk of tired scaffolders making mistakes and causing accidents.

To achieve a planned and organised work pattern, it is necessary to examine existing methods of work. Each task should be analysed:

- What can I do to improve the flow of work?
- What can go wrong?

If the first question had been applied to the first example, a considerable amount of time and effort would not have been wasted. The second question is necessary when planning a work pattern to identify potential hazards. The next example shows how these questions give results that improve productivity and decrease the risks.

Example 2

One further example will serve to show how a thoughtful, commonsense approach to the job can save time and effort and thus reduce the risk of accidents.

In Fig. 11.4 three scaffolders are employed in erecting an independent scaffold.

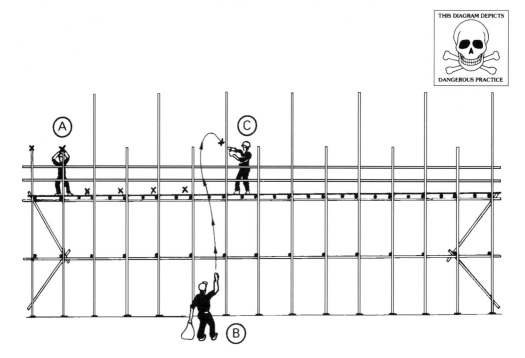

Fig. 11.4

A is fixing right-angle couplers to standards, ready to receive ledgers.

B is throwing up fittings, dragging the sack of fittings along behind.

C is catching the fittings and placing them on the platform, ready for A.

A more efficient use of labour is achieved in the example shown in Fig. 11.5.

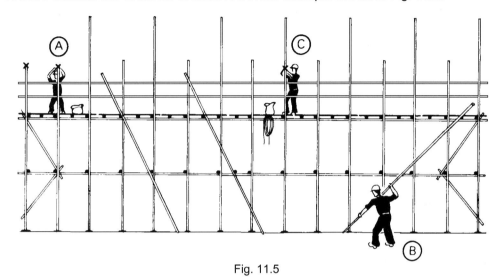

Fig. 11.5

Each of the scaffolders on the platform has their own sack of fittings, which has been raised to the working level with the aid of a light line. The third scaffolder (B) can be employed laying out ledgers ready for fixing. This is obviously a more productive arrangement. Two scaffolders are employed in fixing the couplers instead of one, as in the original example, with the third person preparing for the next stage of the work. The job will proceed more quickly and the risk of someone being injured by a badly thrown or misdirected fitting is eliminated.

Safety note

The common practice of throwing up fittings is efficient only where a small number are required and the distance thrown is not too great. The risk assessment should always be referred to before throwing up fittings. It is far safer to place the fittings in a sack and haul them up to the required level with a line and gin wheel.

It is not intended here to condemn this widespread practice outright; there will be occasions where it is as quick and easy to throw up a few fittings as it is to rig up a gin wheel and line – but it should *never* be done:

- if the scaffold is being erected in a public place
- near glass or near a fragile roof
- anywhere it may cause injury to any person or damage to property
- anywhere other than from ground level
- if the practice contravenes the company's safety policy or the site rules.

Safety and efficiency

These are only two examples of how, with forethought and planning, and by adopting an intelligent approach to the job, scaffolding work can be made easier, less costly and safer. There are many opportunities in scaffolding work to practise these principles. What is needed above all is a thoughtful, conscientious attitude to the job and a concern for safety.

As in so many instances involving scaffolding work, efficiency and safety go hand in hand; efficient working methods are usually also the *safe way* of working.

12. OBSTACLES AND HAZARDS

OVERCOMING OBSTACLES

Many obstacles are encountered in scaffold work, and all present problems that need to be resolved. The solutions may be very simple – for example, raising a ledger to give access to a doorway – or extremely complex – for example, a scaffold bridge over a motorway requiring the expertise of an engineer to design the structure and supervise its construction. In many cases a scaffolder will need to use their own ingenuity in overcoming lesser obstacles.

This chapter offers some advice on how to overcome some of the more typical obstacles encountered in everyday scaffolding operations.

Occupied houses

Many of the problems the scaffolder encounters on this type of job could be overcome by better liaison between the contractor and the householder.

Quite often the householder employs a builder who in turn employs the services of a scaffolding contractor. It is at this point that things can possibly go wrong. The householder may not be told what is going to happen, prior to the scaffolders arriving, and so cannot warn their neighbours, who may already be upset by the general disturbance.

Someone who has just hung out their washing or who has weeded and tidied up the garden will object strongly to the scaffolders laying sole boards over flowerbeds, walking material across the lawn or laying scaffold tubes in the driveway. If access is required through neighbours' grounds, permission is unlikely to be given without prior notice.

Co-operation from both the householder and neighbours will reduce the number of the obstacles the scaffolders will have to face. This can be seen in some of the figures that follow.

(*Note*: guard-rails and bracing have been omitted for clarity.)

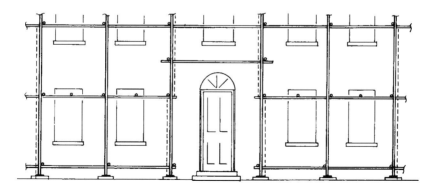

Fig. 12.1

In Fig. 12.1, a simple doorway has been bypassed.

If bridging over a garage roof (Fig. 12.2), can the roof take the weight?

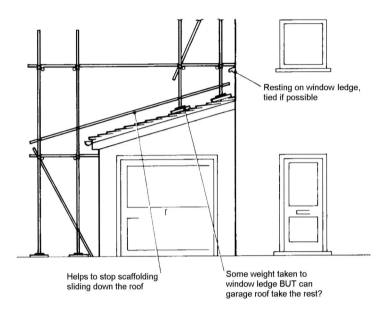

Resting on window ledge, tied if possible

Helps to stop scaffolding sliding down the roof

Some weight taken to window ledge BUT can garage roof take the rest?

Fig. 12.2
(front scaffold omitted for clarity)

Fig. 12.3 shows a lightweight bridge over the garage.

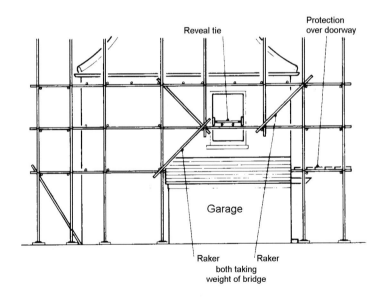

Reveal tie

Protection over doorway

Garage

Raker   Raker
both taking
weight of bridge

Fig. 12.3
(braces, boards, etc., omitted for clarity)

An arrangement for re-roofing that will reduce the amount of wear and tear on the garden and that will also increase productivity is shown in Figs. 12.4 and 12.5.

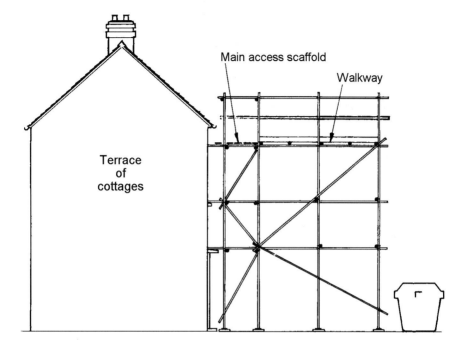

Fig. 12.4
(ladder access and end toe-board omitted for clarity)

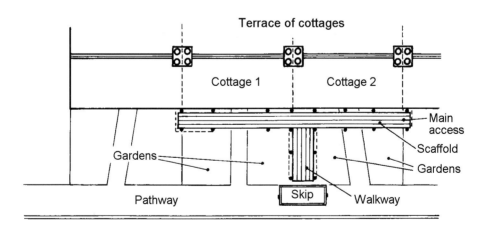

Fig. 12.5

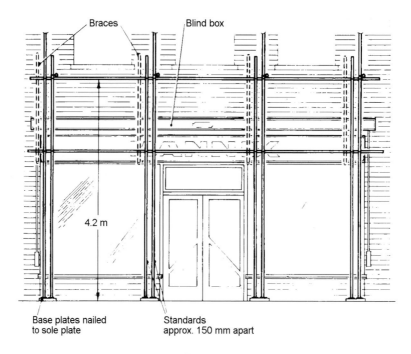

Fig. 12.6
(sway brace omitted for clarity)

Braces   Blind box

4.2 m

Base plates nailed
to sole plate

Standards
approx. 150 mm apart

A typical arrangement on a shop front is shown in Figs. 12.6 and 12.7. The inside standard is founded at first-floor level and the outer standard on the pavement. Generally these scaffolds are for decorators. Occasionally a fan will be added to the scaffold when roofing or chimney work has to be carried out. It may then be necessary to double the outer standards, as shown in Fig.12.7.

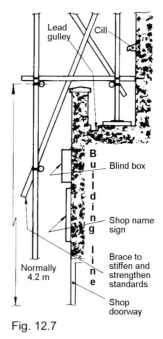

Lead gulley   Cill

Building line

Blind box

Shop name sign

Brace to stiffen and strengthen standards

Normally 4.2 m

Shop doorway

Fig. 12.7

The same principles can be applied to the base of a house that has a basement floor.

Chapter 4 gives examples of typical obstacles scaffolders face.

PUBLIC HAZARDS

Pavement scaffolds cause many problems for the scaffold gang. Materials have to be unloaded and stacked on the pavement or in the gutter, presenting an obstacle and a hazard to others. All local authorities have rules and regulations that must be observed (for example, a pavement licence may be required). It may also be necessary to seek permission from the police to unload lorries in 'No Parking' areas. A risk assessment must be completed to identify possible hazards.

Whenever a scaffold is erected in a busy public place, it is recommended that the local police are kept informed. They can give valuable advice and help in solving many of the problems that may arise. Any warning signs must be proper signs, not home-made ones.

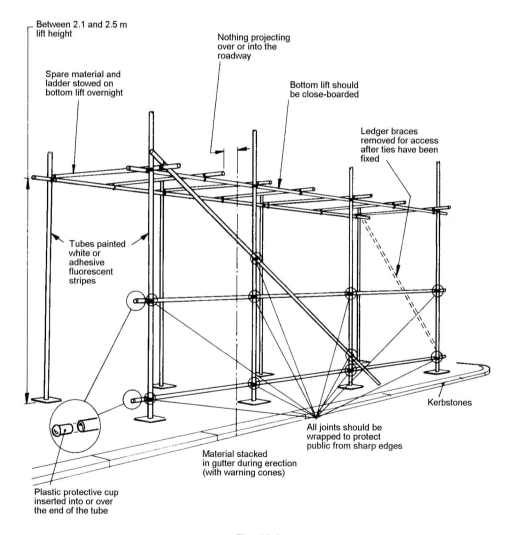

Fig. 12.8

A very important responsibility of all scaffolders is the protection and safety of the public. Particular problems will depend on the scaffold's location: it may be in a busy shopping area, with a narrow pavement adjacent to traffic lights, or near a school, a park or playing area, or pub or fish-and-chip shop. Whatever the location, the following problems will need to be considered:

- At busy and congested sites a very early start will enable the gang to unload the lorry and erect the base of the scaffold before the traffic builds up.

- It may be necessary to remove ledger braces to permit access under the scaffold, and to provide a close-boarded bottom lift to stop anything falling on to pedestrians. If guard-rails or foot tie ledgers are provided, the ends of the tubes should be capped and all joints should be wrapped to prevent injury to passers-by.

- Children tend to be inquisitive and fearless. They will climb ladders or even shin up standards and have a habit of getting themselves into danger. A special watch should be kept when children are out and about after school. Always remove the ladder or attach a scaffold board flat against the rungs of the ladder when leaving the job for lunch or tea breaks to prevent unauthorised access. Any danger areas must be barriered off and warning signs placed in position.

- The evening, night-time and weekends can bring the problems of older children, vandals or adult revellers. All spare material should be secured, either by removing it from the site or stacking it securely on the first lift. Always remove ladders and put them in a safe place – out of reach.

- If through ties have been fixed, someone should ensure that the open window cannot be used by an intruder.

GENERAL SAFETY CONSIDERATIONS

- Safe passage must be provided for the public. Remember that people with visual impairments, wheelchair users, senior citizens and people with shopping trolleys, prams and pushchairs may have difficulty in negotiating places where access is restricted. Barriers should be erected as required.

- No part of the scaffold must project into the roadway where it may be struck by any vehicle.

- Statutory requirements, local authority regulations and police advice should be complied with.

- Lighting regulations must be observed.

- Safety notices must be displayed as necessary.

Other safety considerations

- Projections, such as canopies, large coping stones, bow windows and drainpipes.

- Overhead electricity and telephone cables.

- Fire escapes and emergency exits.

- Foundations.

Considerations prior to dismantling

- Are all the ties intact and secure?

- Have any adaptations taken place and, if so, have they affected the scaffold's stability?

- Has the scaffold been damaged?

- Is there any loose materials or debris on the scaffold?

- If the lighting is fixed to the scaffold, has it been disconnected from the power supply?

13. PROTECTIVE FANS

Fans are erected to afford protection to people below from anything that may fall from a scaffold or building. The Work at Height Regulations require employers to do everything that is reasonably practicable to prevent anything from falling and, when there is no other way of stopping things from falling, then protective fans should be erected and used. If there is a 'danger area' beneath a fan, the area should be barriered off and warning notices displayed.

Fans comprise an inclined framework of scaffold tubes covered with scaffold boards. Fig. 13.1 illustrates the general arrangement.

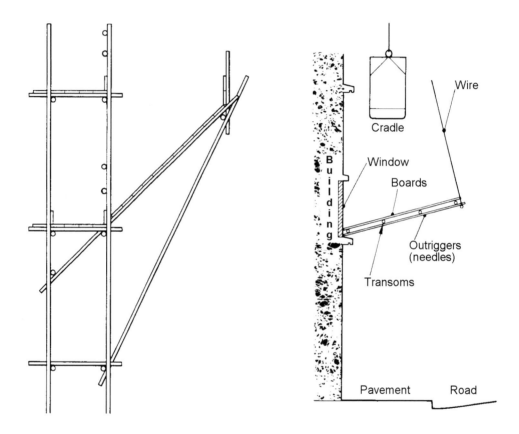

Fig. 13.1

Fans are not intended for access to a scaffold or for the storage of materials. Warning notices to this effect should be clearly displayed on the fan.

> **FANS ARE FOR PROTECTION ONLY**
> **DO NOT USE FOR ACCESS**
> **OR STACKING**

Types of fan

Fans are classified as lightweight or heavyweight according to their load capability. It is not always possible to predict what weight will fall and from what height.

CLASS A   A light-duty fan with a maximum loading equivalent to 0.75 kN/m², suitable for protection from paint and mortar droppings.

CLASS B   A medium-duty fan with a maximum loading equivalent to 1 kN/m², for protection from bricks, aggregates and like weights from heights not exceeding 10 m.

CLASS C   A fan with a loading over 1 kN/m² to prevent objects larger than bricks falling more than 10 m. They must be designed to suit the application.

CLASS D   A fan for arresting the fall of persons or falling materials from a height of 6 m or two storeys. This is usually a safety net system and should be in accordance with BS EN 1263-1 1997 (*Safety Nets. Safety Requirements – Test Methods*) and rigged in accordance with BS EN 1263-2 (*Safety Requirements for the Positioning Limits*).

Design and construction

Fans in Classes A and B may be specifically designed, although the standard form may be constructed without design drawings to a recognised standard configuration. Fans in Classes C and D must be professionally designed and are beyond the scope of this book.

Fans attached to scaffolds

Fans consist of outriggers or needles extended from the scaffold, supported by wires or spurs (rakers). Transoms are run parallel with the scaffold ledgers to permit the fan to be boarded or sheeted at right angles to the building or scaffold. A common method of fixing light-duty fans is to pass the outriggers over the outside ledger and under the inside one. The problems of this arrangement are shown in Fig. 13. 2. In any event, it is better not to fix fans to existing lift ledgers.

1. Additional loading on inside ledger might cause uplift – although unlikely.

2. Likelihood of materials being placed on the fan. Difficulty of removing debris via working lift.

3. Wire support can cause falling materials to bounce off and miss the fan. Wire may also be damaged.

4. Shallow angle allows falling material to build up on the outside edge of the fan. Removal of this poses a safety hazard to people on the fan.

5. Handrails erected on the outside edge of the fan encourage personnel to walk on the fan, thus increasing fan loading.

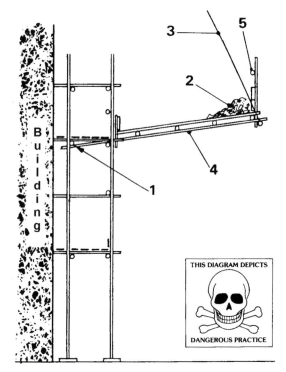

THIS DIAGRAM DEPICTS

DANGEROUS PRACTICE

Fig. 13.2

Fans attached to buildings (Class A)

These are generally used in conjunction with cradles for window cleaning, stone-cleaning operations or other maintenance work on the face of the building. The suspension points for the cradle and the wire for supports may often be the same. Large quantities of water are often required for these jobs. In these circumstances, corrugated sheeting is usually fixed so as to afford adequate and safe drainage.

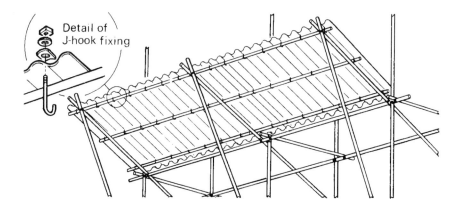

Detail of J-hook fixing

Fig. 13.3

General construction requirements

Outriggers (**needles**) should be spaced every 1.5 m for fans attached to buildings, and every bay when attached to scaffolds. Class B fans should be fixed at every scaffold bay.

Support transoms must be spaced so as to make sure there are no 'traps' in the decking.

Parapets should be erected by fixing puncheons on the outside fan ledger and fixing toe-boards to these.

Spurs and **rakers** are generally described as transom supports if used to support the fan from above instead of wires. The term 'spurs' is generally employed to describe raking tubes used to support the fan from below. Spurs should be fixed to the outside fan ledger or an additional ledger within the outside third of the fan.

Wires The diameter and strength of suspension wires should be designed according to the size and loading of the fan. Most purpose-made slinging wire is 8 mm independent wire rope core (IWRC), which has a breaking strain of 4 tonnes but a safe working load of 0.5 tonnes. Wires should be fixed using a round turn and three bulldog grips. **ON NO ACCOUNT SHOULD 6 mm DIAMETER WIRE LASHINGS BE USED.**

Additional ties must be fixed at the level of the fan (see Chapter 5); only load-bearing fittings may be used in their construction. Large fans supported by spurs will require additional bracing.

Decking

When erecting a fan it is important to make sure that the lift at the level at which the fan is fixed is boarded out so that material does not fall down the inside of the scaffold. Alternative arrangements may be made (for example, parapets fixed to the inside of the fan, or the next lift down boarded out).

Scaffold boards should either be lashed, using 6 mm wire, or secured with an additional scaffold tube. Galvanised corrugated iron sheets may also be fixed using tubes, with a variety of sheeting clips round the edge of the sheets or with sheeting hooks that pass through the sheets and hook round the supporting scaffold tubes.

Fans are often exposed to high winds that have the potential to lift sheets and boards off the fan. Consequently, it is important to make sure that all decking is **firmly secured**.

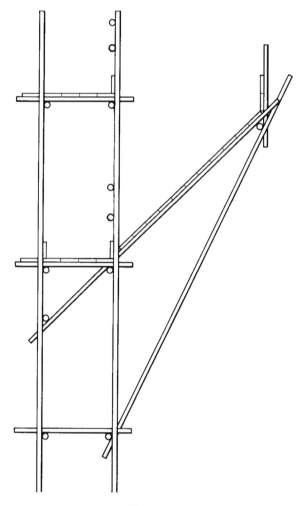

Fig. 13.4

SAFETY CHECK

- Spacing of outriggers to suit the load on the fan (i.e. type of decking and duty of fan).

- Scaffold must be:
  – close boarded
  – properly lashed or held down
  – properly supported (i.e. no 'traps').

- Corrugated sheeting must:
  – have a minimum of four clips or hook bolts per sheet
  – drain properly. Guttering and drainpipes must be fixed where necessary

- Fan should be inspected by the user and particular care taken after high winds and storms. Any damage to the fan must be repaired immediately.

94

Part 2
Basic Scaffold Structures

14. INDEPENDENT TIED SCAFFOLDS

The independent tied scaffold is perhaps the most commonly used scaffold. It consists of two rows of standards parallel to the building, joined together with ledgers fixed with right-angle couplers. In turn, transoms are fixed at right angles to the ledgers with 'putlog' couplers. The assembly must be braced with ledger bracing, usually at alternate pairs of standards, and with longitudinal or facade bracing, which can be along the entire face of the scaffold or at least at every five bays, and across one bay or two bays for the entire height of the scaffold. Independent scaffolds must be tied to the building (see Chapter 5, page 29).

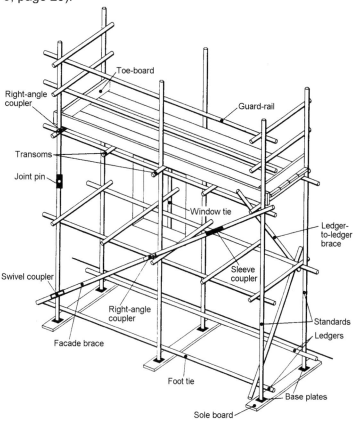

Fig. 14.1

Uses and loadings

The uses to which independent scaffolds may be put and their associated permissible loadings are summarised in Table 2.1 (see page 14).

Most independent scaffolds are five boards wide with four boards between the standards and one board between the inside standard and the building. Two and three-- board scaffolds are used when there is restricted access between buildings or for inspection purposes only. Strength and stability calculations and an engineering design by a competent scaffold engineer are required for independent scaffolds unless such calculations are already available (perhaps from a previous scaffold) and the scaffold is being built to a generally recognised standard configuration.

The requirements for bracing and tying independent scaffolds have been discussed in other chapters; however, these are summarised below for convenience:

- Longitudinal bracing along the face of the scaffold, either continuous or 'dog-leg'.

- Ledger bracing at alternate pairs of standards, using right-angle couplers from ledger to ledger or swivel couplers to standards.

- Ties should be every other lift and approximately every bay along the scaffold. Not more than half the ties should be reveal ties.

ACCESS

The main working platform for independent scaffolds can often be 30–40 m above the ground. Consequently, access of persons and materials to this platform requires careful consideration. Materials are often raised by hoists, but scaffolders and others normally gain access via ladders. For higher working platforms (above 20 m), a ladder tower is preferred, and this gives access to each lift if required.

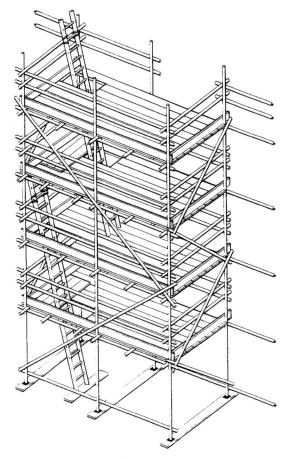

Fig. 14.2

Alternatively, ladders and landings can be built into the scaffold itself. The distance between landings must not be more than 9 m. Access holes through landings should not be more than 500 mm wide and should be as small as practicable in the other direction. Ladders should project a suitable distance above each landing (usually five rungs or 1 m), unless some other suitable handhold is available. They should be set at an angle of 4 vertical to 1 horizontal and supported only by the stiles, which should be secured at the top using lashings or proprietary fixings.

ROUTINE SAFETY CHECK

Each night

- Ladders should be removed or boarded up to prevent unauthorised access to the scaffold.

- Lights should be placed so that the public are protected from accidentally damaging themselves or the scaffold (for example, by driving into it).

- Check that warning signs are in position.

Each morning

- Make sure that the scaffold has not been interfered with, particularly by children, and is safe for use.

Every week

- Statutory inspections must be made by a 'competent person' at least every seven days and after storms or any other conditions likely to jeopardise the scaffold's safety. A report of inspection must be prepared covering the following points:

  - The name and address of the person for whom the inspection was carried out.
  - The location of the scaffold(s) inspected.
  - A description of the scaffold(s) inspected.
  - The date and time of the inspection.
  - Details of any matter identified that could give rise to a risk to the health and safety of any person (i.e. defects in the scaffold).
  - Details of any action taken as a result of the above.
  - Details of any further action considered necessary.
  - The name and position of the person making the report.
  - However, if a scaffold has been 'handed over' to a client, then it is the client's responsibility to ensure that the scaffold is inspected, although they may contract the scaffold company to carry out the inspections on their behalf.

When dismantling

- The order in which a scaffold is dismantled is not necessarily the reverse of the order of erection. Generally, scaffolds should be taken down lift by lift and not from one end to the other. However, reference should of course be made to the scaffold plan or design, and the risk assessment or work instructions.

Hazard awareness

Independent scaffolds are in common use and are often taken for granted. While independent scaffolds are straightforward to erect and use, carelessness can result in accidents. An awareness of the potential hazards is essential if accidents are to be avoided.

ERECTING AN INDEPENDENT SCAFFOLD

Fig. 14.3 shows a typical sequence of erection (for a three-person gang). (Right-angle coupler is abbreviated to RAC.) In some of the figures different activities are shown, but the sequence is always A, B, C.

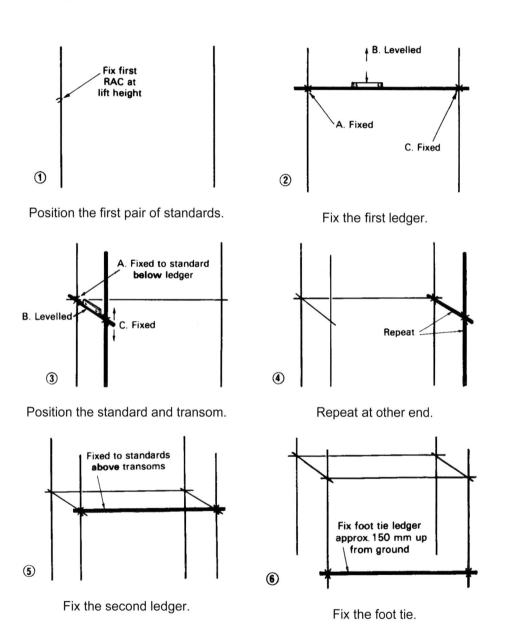

Fig. 14.3

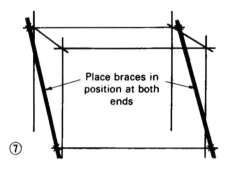

Place braces in position at both ends

⑦

Attach the braces and check the structure is plumb and level.

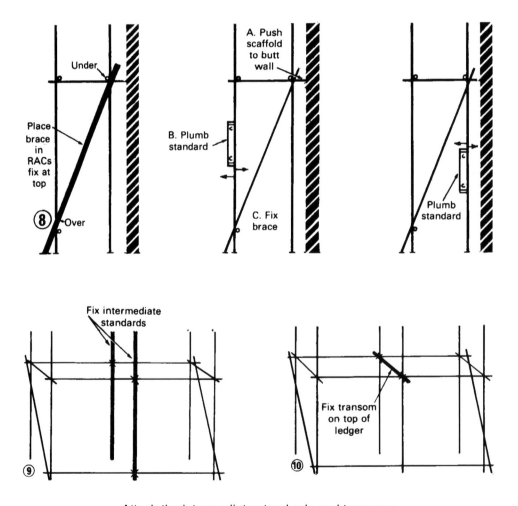

Attach the intermediate standards and transoms.

Fig. 14.4

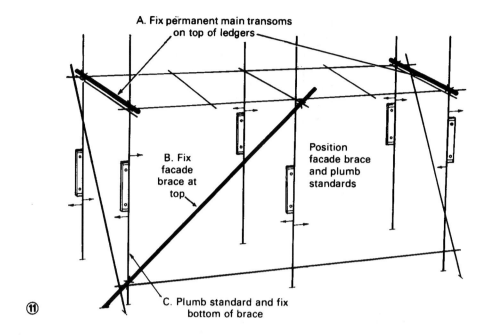

A. Fix permanent main transoms on top of ledgers

B. Fix facade brace at top

Position facade brace and plumb standards

C. Plumb standard and fix bottom of brace

⑪

Plumb the remaining standards and fix the intermediate transoms to suit the boards.

Fig. 14.4 (cont'd)

Boards, guard-rails and toe-boards, as necessary, would then be fitted to the first lift as the scaffolders progressed upwards. These will be left in place or some of the materials removed for use elsewhere in the scaffold.

15. PUTLOG SCAFFOLDS

The putlog scaffold, also called a bricklayer's scaffold, is erected with tubes and fittings to support a work platform adjacent to a wall or building.

The scaffold consists of a single row of standards parallel to the face of the wall, supported and tied together by a ledger. The ledger also supports the outer end of the putlog, the other end of which is inserted into the wall.

The putlog is, in effect, a transom that has been flattened at one end to form a blade; alternatively, the transom may have a putlog adaptor connected at one end. The blade is fully inserted into the bed joint of the brickwork or laid flat on top of the brickwork; alternatively, when the scaffold is erected against existing brickwork, it may be inserted on its edge into a vertical joint.

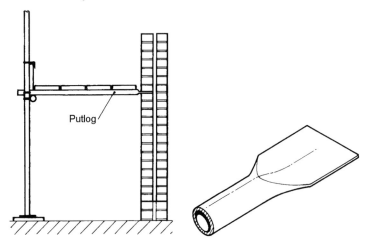

Putlog

Fig. 15.1

CONSTRUCTION

Standards

These should be placed on base plates, founded on sole boards. The spacing between standards should not exceed 2.1 m with a maximum distributed load of 2.0 kN/m². The lift height is normally 1.35 m.

Ties

Through ties must be inserted on alternate lifts to the full height of the scaffold and every other bay horizontally. On progressive bricklayer's scaffolds, care must be taken when the brickwork is 'green'. The scaffold should not be worked on until the brickwork is capable of supporting the scaffold.

It must be remembered that a putlog fitting is not a tie. On walls without openings single bricks should be left out to accept ties.

Bracing

Facade or sway braces must be fixed in the normal way. Ledger or cross braces are not strictly required although, for a progressive bricklayer's scaffold it is advisable to fit a ledger brace every second standard.

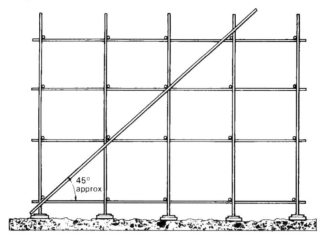

Fig. 15.2

Bridle tube

Where it is necessary to bypass a window or door opening, a bridle tube is connected to the underside of the putlogs to act as a support for the ends of putlogs not supported by the brickwork. It should be fixed with right-angle couplers.

The bridle tube also serves as the inner fixing point for braces.

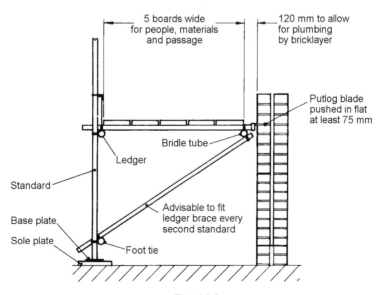

Fig. 15.3

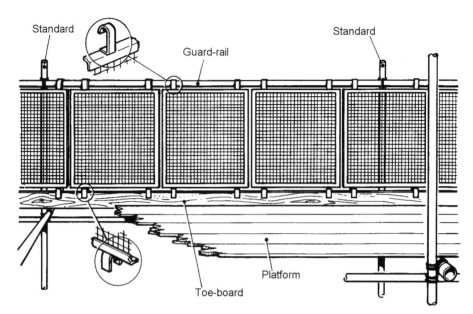

Fig. 15.4

Fig. 15.5

Working platform

The working platform should be five boards wide, with sufficient room between the face of the brickwork and the edge of the inside board to allow the bricklayer to plumb the brickwork. The gap also allows for the superfluous mortar to drop to the ground without spoiling the face of the brickwork.

In addition to the normal arrangement of guard-rails and toe-boards, brick-guards should be erected to ensure material cannot fall from the platform.

Guard-rails and toe-boards are of course fixed on the inside of the standards and the brick-guards are then hung on the inside of the guard-rail and toe-board so that they cannot swing outwards if someone falls against them.

Note: The end guard-rail is not shown in Fig. 15.5.

HAZARDS

Some of the hazards more commonly associated with putlog scaffolds are listed below:

- Foundations can be undermined by other work, or the scaffold might have been erected on backfilled trenches.

- Working platforms can be overloaded and might have bricks stacked higher than the guard-rail.

- The guard-rails are removed for fork-lift access and not replaced.

- Toe-boards are sometimes removed and used to prop up door or window frames.

- Single unsupported boards are used to provide access to the brick stack.

- Brick-guards have not been erected (or are not available).

- Ties or have been braces removed.

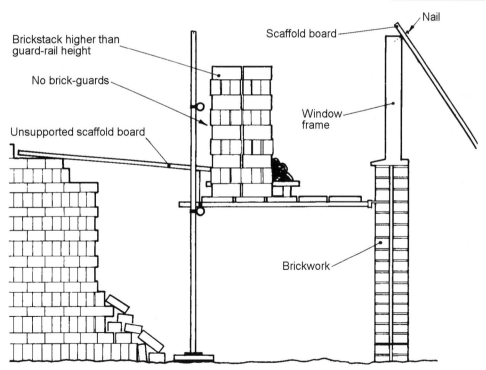

Fig. 15.6

ERECTION SEQUENCE

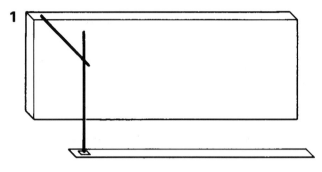

Fig. 15.7

Erect the standard on the sole board and base plate and fix the first putlog to the standard with a right-angle coupler.

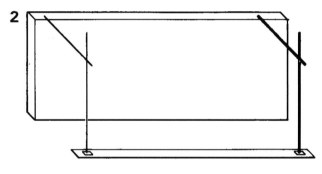

Fig. 15.8

Fix the second standard and putlog as before.

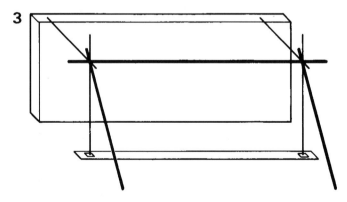

Fig. 15.9

Fix the ledger to the standards below the putlogs. The structure is temporarily supported with rakers.

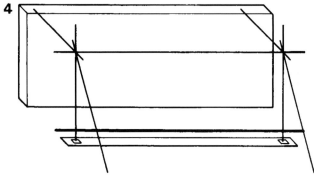

Fig. 15.10

Level and fix the foot tie ledger approximately 150 mm above the base plate.

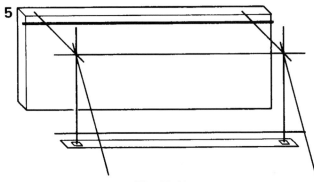

Fig. 15.11

Fix the bridle tube approximately 100 mm from the wall.

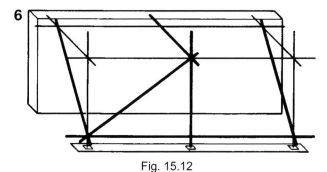

Fig. 15.12

Brace the structure. Ledger braces may be fixed from the bridle to the foot tie, including the facade brace, to provide longitudinal stability.

The scaffold is completed by adding intermediate transoms, the working platform and guard-rails and toe-boards.

SAFETY CHECKLIST

Before erection

- Clear all debris and level the ground.
- Ensure all backfilled trenches are firmly compacted.
- Ensure the scaffolder is aware of the backfilled trench positions.
- Ensure the scaffolder is aware of the position of future groundworks.

After erection of base lift

- Standards plumb and properly founded on sole boards and base plates.
- Ledgers level and connected to the standards by well-serviced right-angle couplers.
- Putlog ends (or putlog adaptors) are properly inserted into, or laid on the brickwork.
- Putlogs are level, properly spaced and connected to the ledgers (the main putlogs within 300 mm of each standard).
- Bridles are connected to the putlogs with right-angle couplers.
- Boards are close laid and properly supported and sufficient space has been allowed between the inner edge and the face of the brickwork to allow the bricklayer to plumb the wall.
- Guard-rails, toe-boards and brick-guards are in place.
- Proper access has been provided in the **correct** position (normally adjacent to the brick stack, and the mixer).

Ensure the bricklayer, foreman and the fork-lift driver are aware of the maximum loads the scaffold is capable of carrying (for example,

- 2.1 m standard spacing = 2.0 kN/m² which, in turn, equals approximately 110 bricks (stacked next to each standard), one loaded mortar board and the bricklayer and their tools – per bay).

After the erection of the second lift and before it is boarded out:

- Ensure the ties have been fixed to **mature** brickwork.

Generally, it is impossible to fix ties to the second lift without leaving holes in the brickwork, and second-lift brickwork is unlikely to be mature enough to provide a secure tie. Ties should be inserted in the **base lift to mature brickwork** (i.e. through door and window openings).

- Ensure the blades of the putlogs are still fully inserted in the wall, at base lift level. There is a tendency for scaffolders to 'spring' the scaffold away from the building when inserting the second-lift putlogs. This is less likely to occur if ledger braces are incorporated.

During operations, ensure:

- The fork-lift driver does not overload the platforms.

- Brick-guards are always used.

- Unused ladder access points are properly guarded.

- Any damage done by the fork-lift or dumpers is rectified immediately.

- Boards are not taken and used as props for door frames, window frames and roof trusses.

- Gable ends have proper through ties.

- The gable-end lifts have **correctly supported** boards, guard-rails and toe-boards, and proper access and egress.

If the scaffold is to be used for roof tiling, ensure:

- The top lift is high enough for the tiler to step comfortably on to the roof.

- The tiler cannot fall over the scaffold guard-rail if they fall down the roof (if necessary, consider fixing additional guard-rails).

During progressive dismantling, ensure:

- The guard-rails are erected at the correct height and the platform is properly laid for the bricklayer who is pointing up the putlog holes or replacing bricks where through ties have been used.

- The ties are left in place until it is safe to remove them.

16. BIRDCAGE ACCESS SCAFFOLDS

The 'birdcage' scaffold is so called because it resembles a cage! It is normally used inside buildings to provide a platform for working on ceilings or soffits or for the installation of lighting, ventilation or sprinkler systems. Small jobs are generally done using a tower or hydraulically operated aerial platform but, for larger projects involving longer periods of time, a birdcage scaffold is required.

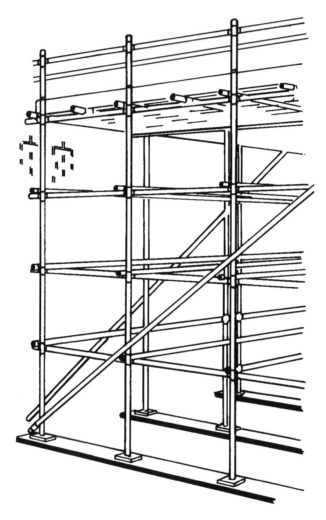

Fig. 16.1

The scaffold is constructed using standards arranged at regular intervals in parallel lines, usually evenly spaced. Standards are laced together with a grid of ledgers and transoms at every lift height and the top lift is boarded out to provide the working platform.

112

SCAFFOLD REQUIREMENTS

The specifications for birdcage access scaffolds are fully set out in the NASC guide and vary according to whether the birdcage is single lift or more than one lift. Service class 1 (with a loading capacity of 0.75kN/m^2) is the most common configuration and, where a larger imposed load is required, the scaffold needs to be specially designed.

For single-lift birdcages, particular attention must be paid to bracing. These requirements are summarised below:

Maximum loading
0.75 kN/m² (equivalent to one person every square metre).

Standard spacing
Maximum 2.1 m in each direction.

Lift heights
First lift maximum 2.5 m, subsequent lifts maximum 2.0 m.

Edge bays
The width of the edge bays may be three, four or five boards to accommodate the access requirements for the scaffold.

Ledgers, transoms and fittings
Ledgers and transoms should be fixed to standards and to each other with right-angle couplers. At the working lift, transoms may be fixed to ledgers with putlog clips to enable boards to be laid.

Bracing
Braces may be fixed from ledger to ledger or to standards using swivel couplers. When ledger bracing is used, a foot tie is required to receive the lower end of the brace on the first lift. One brace must be provided for every five bays in each line in both directions (either zig-zag or diagonal). If the birdcage scaffold is fully butted at all levels, then braces can be omitted.

Tying and butting
Stability may also be provided by butting tubes against existing structures. However, if only one wall is available it is necessary to provide a push-pull fixing. Where two parallel walls are available, tubes can be butted against both walls (in which case timber packing and reveal screws can be used). No vertical should be more than six tubes away from an edge or other restraint point.

CONSTRUCTION

Foundations

Great care must be taken when scaffolds are erected on polished wood block, mosaic, marble and similar floors. If necessary a protective layer of suitable material must be placed under the sole boards.

With birdcage scaffolds the floor of the building has to carry the full weight of the scaffold and its load, and the design should take this into account. Sole boards are therefore necessary to help distribute the load as widely as possible – and they should always be set at right angles to beams or joists.

Base plates and standards

Base plates must be placed on sole boards to receive standards. These should be nailed or screwed to the sole boards if there is any danger of movement. Standards should be plumbed, and joints in alternate standards should be staggered in order to gain strength and stability.

Ledgers

At all times, ledgers should be fixed in a horizontal plane. The recommendation is that the first lift should be fitted at a height of 2.5 m, and the subsequent lifts at 2 m maximum.

Transoms

On non-working lifts, transoms should be fixed to the standards by right-angle couplers. On working lifts, transoms should be fixed to the ledgers with right-angle or putlog couplers and spaced as other scaffolds to support the boards evenly (see Table 2.3 on page 15.)

Generally, one transom should be fixed in each bay, not more than 300 mm from a standard. Joints in transoms must be staggered in order to obtain maximum rigidity and safety.

Bracing

Stability is obtained by diagonally bracing to the full height of the scaffold at each corner and in both directions, particularly if it is not possible to include ties (see 'Scaffold requirements' on the previous page).

Ties

Tying is normally achieved by butting walls with alternate ledgers and transoms. (The ends of tube may have to be padded to prevent damage.) Alternatively, box or reveal ties may be necessary. Foot ties should be provided throughout the scaffold except where access is required, and at least in alternate bays in both directions to form boxes.

Working platform

The working platform must be close boarded a minimum of 600 mm wide and, if 3.9 m boards are used, each board must span at least four transoms. Hand-rails and toe-boards must be provided where the space between the decking and the wall exceeds 150 mm. These must be fitted on the *inside* of the standards.

Access

Safe access must be provided on to the working platform, which is usually by ladder to one edge of the platform. If the access is up through the scaffold platform, suitable and sufficient precautions must be taken to prevent people from falling through the access hole while working (see 'Access' on page 44).

METHODS OF ERECTION

The usual method of erection for a birdcage scaffold is to fix a foot tie around a box two bays wide, approximately 150 mm from the base, fixed to the standards at each of the four corners, and then followed by ledgers at the first-lift height. Intermediate standards and braces are then fitted.

Erect standards at each corner and secure with foot ties (Fig. 16.2).

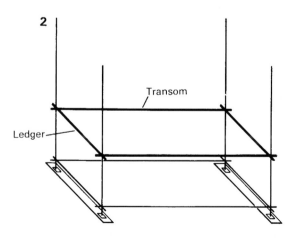

Fig. 16.2

Attach ledgers and transoms at the first lift, ensuring the standards are plumb (Fig. 16.3).

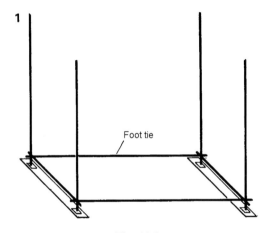

Fig. 16.3

Insert intermediate standards and ledgers (Fig. 16.4).

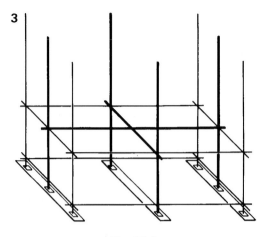

Fig. 16.4

Fix facade braces at each corner (Fig. 16.5).

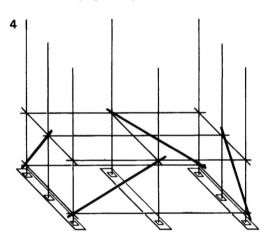

Fig. 16.5

Fix the centre standard (Fig. 16.6).

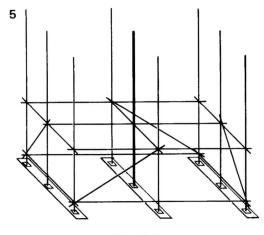

Fig. 16.6

Attach temporary transoms and board out scaffold to work from for next lift, putting guard-rails in place as necessary (Fig. 16.7).

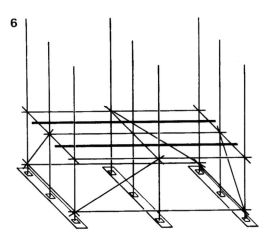

Fig. 16.7
(boards and guard-rails not shown for clarity)

Attach the ledgers for the second lift (Fig. 16.8).

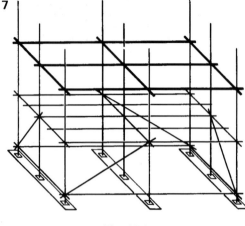

Fig. 16.8

Continue the facade bracing in a zig-zag or dog-leg fashion (Fig. 16.9).

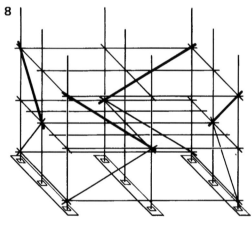

Fig. 16.9

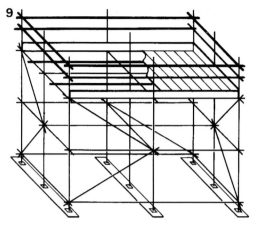

Fig. 16.10

This sequence is repeated until the structure is at the required height. The working platform will then be boarded-out and guard-rails and toe-boards fitted.

Safety checklist

- The sole boards are positioned so that the total weight is distributed as widely as possible. The base plates of the standards are secured to sole boards.

- The standards are not more than 2.1 m apart in each direction, are vertical and in line.

- The ledgers are level and in line (also the spacing of the transoms).

- The diagonal bracing in both directions is securely fixed with swivel couplers.

- The security of the ties, where used. Where transoms or ledgers butt the wall, check there is no gap. Packing may be needed to prevent damage to the wall.

- The security and condition of boards, toe-boards and guard-rails.

- The security of couplers and fittings, and also the condition of fittings.

- The load on the working platform is evenly spread – the platform must not be overloaded. Materials should be stacked near standards. Where necessary, such things as brick-guards must be used.

- The ladders provided for access are correctly supported or secured and extend at least 1 m or five rungs above platform level, unless another suitable handhold is available.

17. TOWER SCAFFOLDS

The NASC guide gives four classifications for tower scaffolds:
   a)   light duty for use inside buildings
   b)   light duty for use in the open
   c)   heavy duty
   d)   protection structures.

The following text relates only to light-duty towers in classes a and b, with a service class 2 loading of 1.5 kN/m^2.

When scaffold towers are formed from standard-steel scaffold tube and fittings, they may be fitted with castors or wheels for mobility or constructed as stationary towers. They usually support a single working platform not projecting beyond the base area, and they are provided with hand-rails and toe-boards. Access to the working platform by ladder may be either inside or outside the structure.

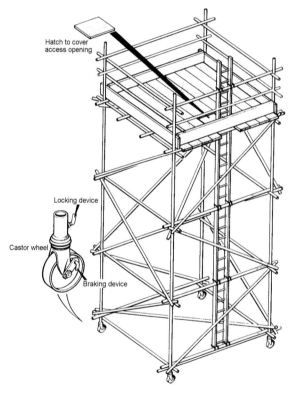

Hatch to cover
access opening

Locking device

Castor wheel

Braking device

Fig. 17.1
(measurements shown for illustrative purposes only)

Note: Proprietary towers in both steel and aluminium are not covered in this chapter. These should be constructed (or erected) and used strictly in accordance with the manufacturer's or supplier's instructions. Typical construction of a tower scaffold is shown. Design calculations are required for all towers.

Light-duty access towers (**classes a and b**) are used mainly for such lightweight work as painting and simple maintenance, and will not support a load greater than 1.5 kN/m². This is equivalent to a load of two people standing per square metre. The safe working load should be clearly displayed on the working platform. These may be stationary or mobile.

Heavy-duty towers (**class c**), such as camera towers and welding platforms, must be capable of sustaining distributed loads in excess of this figure. These towers are nearly always stationary, and expert advice should be sought in their design and erection.

Protection structures (**class d**), such as for power-line crossings.

Foundations

Scaffold towers must always be vertical, even if erected on sloping ground.

Mobile scaffold towers should only be used and moved on firm and level surfaces. Where the ground is uneven or soft, it may be necessary to lay a temporary foundation or track to spread the weight and permit the tower to be moved more easily and safely. These temporary foundations should be suitably constructed so that the bearing capacity of the ground immediately below the track is not exceeded at any point. Any displacement of the foundation or track should be prevented by anchoring it securely.

The anchoring of the track to the ground does not negate the necessity for the tower itself to be anchored to the ground where this is essential.

Where it is known that a tower is to be used on a suspended floor, it should be designed so that the load is no greater than the bearing capacity of the floor. Expert advice should be sought in these circumstances.

When guy wires are used or kentledge (ballast weight) is applied to provide stability, the load imposed on the standards is considerably increased. The foundations must be capable of supporting these increased loads.

The general rules relating to foundations apply equally to stationary towers. On some sites, adjustable base plates may be needed to ensure the tower is vertical. These must be prevented from falling out of the vertical tubes, and any locking devices must be correctly engaged.

Height and stability

To give stability to a tower the ratio of the righting moment (the force acting to keep the tower upright) to the overturning moment (wind forces or an eccentric weight such as that imposed by a gin wheel) should be greater than 1.5. In practice this is achieved by limiting the height to the least base ratio. Outriggers may be used to increase the stability of a tower, by effectively increasing the base dimensions.

The height to least base dimension ratio of mobile access towers used within buildings, and with a maximum height of 12 m, should not exceed 3.5 to 1. Mobile access towers used outside (or adjacent to) buildings, and with a maximum height of 8 m, should have a ratio not more than 3 to 1. No tower should be built with a least base dimension of less than 1.2 m. Towers in excess of the 12 m and 8 m height limits should be specifically designed by a scaffold engineer.

For stationary towers these ratios may be increased to 4 to 1 and 3.5 to 1 respectively. These ratios apply only to towers constructed of steel scaffolding materials. (Aluminium towers are lighter and different criteria apply.)

The height to base ratios are summarised below:

	Inside buildings		Outside buildings	
	Height limit	Height to base ratio	Height limit	Height to base ratio
Static tower	12 m	4 to 1	8 m	3.5 to 1
Mobile tower	12 m	3.5 to 1	8 m	3 to 1

The height is measured from the ground (floor) to the level of the working platform.

Towers should be braced on all sides and in plan at every alternate lift, beginning at the base and also under deck level.

Anchors and guys

To increase the stability of stationary towers, guy ropes may be fixed to the tower and attached to anchors founded in the ground. There are four common types:

- Cross tubes attached to the foot lift.

- Driven tube anchors attached to guys.

- Screwed-in flight anchors.

- Plate and pin anchors.

Guys for temporary scaffolding structures should be of 10 mm or 12 mm-diameter wire rope, which should be attached to the scaffold structure and to the ground tube or anchored by a single round turn and three bulldog clips.

Detailed descriptions and methods of use for anchors and guys are not covered in this book but are to be found in the NASC guide.

Castors

Suitable castors or wheels should be selected to suit the tower's size and loading. The safe working load is usually marked on the wheels. These must be fixed at the extreme corners of the tower in such a manner that they cannot fall out if the tower is moved, or a wheel is out of contact with the ground. They must be fitted with effective wheel brakes that cannot be released accidentally.

When a dead weight (such as sand bags and concrete blocks) is used to stabilise a tower, the castors' capacity to take the extra load should be checked.

Ladder access

Ladders should be fixed by lashing the ladder's stiles to horizontal tubes, and should be located on the narrower face of the tower. Unless it is not practicable, ladders must be positioned inside the base area. When the means of access is outside the structure, consideration should be given to the effect on the tower's stability.

Where the ladder is on the inside, access must be provided through the platform (see also page 44), and a hinged or replaceable cover provided for the opening. If the ladder is on the outside, a hinged hand-rail section must be provided to ensure safe access. However, the use of external ladders is not encouraged by the Health and Safety Executive.

TOWER CONSTRUCTION

The height of the lifts should not exceed 2.7 m. The lowest ledgers and transoms should be fixed as near to the castors as possible. The tower should be stiffened using diagonal bracing at approximately 45° to the horizontal on all four faces. Ledgers, transoms and plain braces must be joined to the standards by right-angle couplers. Standards should be joined with sleeve couplers or lapped tubes, never with internal spigot pins. All joints should be staggered.

The minimum base dimension is 1.2 m. When the tower base is greater than 2.5 m x 2.5 m, the tower's weight hinders it from being moved easily and, for these larger towers, design advice should be sought.

The working platform

Working platforms should be close boarded with toe-boards and double safety rails. Transoms should be spaced at intervals not exceeding 1.2 m when 38 mm thick scaffold boards are used. Where short boards are used (for example at access openings), they must be fixed down at both ends to prevent tipping. It is good practice to do this for all boards.

USE

The user should never apply horizontal forces at the level of the working platform (for example, by hauling on ropes or cables) and should not lift significant weights up the outside of the tower. Where gin wheels are used on cantilevered tubes the tower must be specially designed for this purpose.

Mobile towers should only be used on level ground, never on a slope that may allow them to run away. Castors should be locked except when the tower is being moved. If there is any doubt about the adequacy of the brakes, wheels should be checked and, if necessary, replaced.

Mobile towers should never be moved with people or materials on the working platform. When moving the tower, this should be done by pushing at the lowest practical point.

ERECTION SEQUENCE

The erection sequence for a Tower Scaffold is shown on pages 126–7.

Safety checklist

Foundations

- Ensure that the ground surface is firm and level.
- For stationary towers check that the standards are fitted with base plates and that the base plates are securely fixed to prevent lateral movement.
- If temporary foundations or pathways have been provided for a mobile tower, see that they are properly prepared.
- Ensure that suspended floors are not overloaded.
- Check for additional loads that may be imposed when guys or ballast weights are used.

Standards

- Standards must be vertical and stable.
- Joints should be made with sleeve couplers and staggered.

Ledgers and transoms

- These must be horizontal and complete.
- They must be fitted to standards with right-angle couplers.
- The lowest ledgers and transoms fixed as near to castors as possible.
- The spacing of transoms should be 1.2 m or less.

Bracing

- Towers are braced on all sides and in plan at every alternate lift starting at the base lift and also under deck level.

Ladders

- Check that the ladder is lashed top and bottom on each stile. The ladder should be fixed to the narrower side of the tower.
- Ensure that the foot of the ladder is about 150 mm clear of the castor so that the tower can be moved about easily.

Working platform

- Only one working platform is permitted.
- The decking must be in good condition and be evenly supported with the correct overhang.
- Where ladder access is provided, there must be only a minimum gap for access to the working platform.

Guard-rails and toe-boards

- These must be in place and properly secured.

Couplers

- Check that only the correct couplers are used and that they are fully tightened.

Tubes

- Check all tubes for splits, flattened ends and corrosion.

Castors

- Ensure that the castors are fitted so that they cannot fall off if out of contact with the ground.
- Check that the brakes are fitted and are in proper working order.
- Check the castors are greased regularly and rotate freely.
- Check the wheel treads are in good condition.

Loading

- Ensure that the maximum distributed load is not greater than 1.5 kN/m² and that where kentledge is used to ensure stability, the castors are capable of supporting the load.

Ties and guying

- The guys should be checked to ensure that the tension is correct and that the connecting points and anchors are secure.
- On larger towers, seek advice on the methods of guying and on the loads imposed by guys and ties.

Note: Towers must be secured against such things as adverse weather, trespass and vandalism when left unattended.

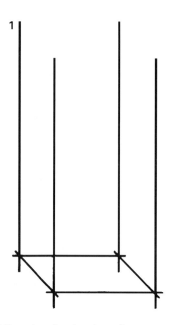

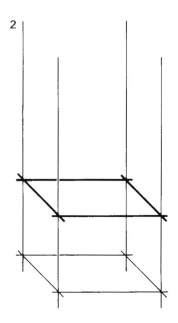

Erect the standards at each corner and secure to the foot tie.

Measure off the first lift and fix the ledgers and transoms, level and secured with right-angle couplers. Ensure that the standards are plumb.

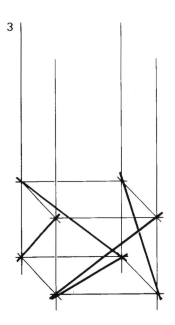

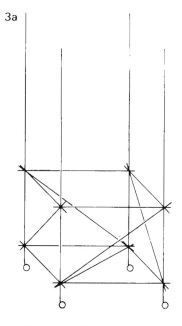

Add braces on all four sides and fix the plan brace

For mobile towers fit castors, secure and brake.

Fig. 17.2

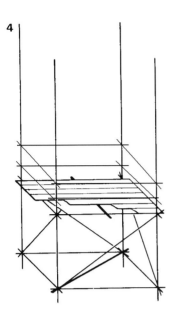

Fix the intermediate transoms, deck out the temporary intermediate working platform and fit the temporary guard-rails.

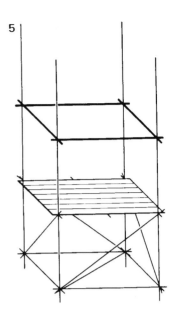

Measure off the second lift and fit the ledgers and transoms (temporary guard-rails not shown in 5, 6 and 7 for clarity).

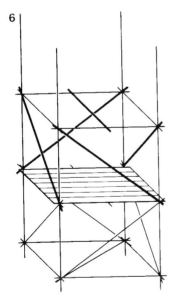

Add the braces and intermediate transoms.

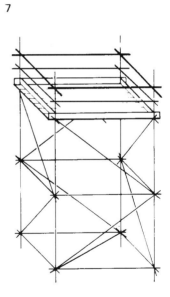

Board out the working platform and add the guard-rails and toe-boards.

Fig. 17.2 (cont'd.)

18. SYSTEM SCAFFOLDS

Introduction

System scaffolding may be described as 'easy-to-use' scaffolding that can be assembled by employees who are not scaffolders but who have received the appropriate instruction and training in the correct assembly of that type of system scaffold. A great many such systems are now available, ranging from light-duty aluminium alloy access towers to heavy-duty steel support structures. They all employ different patented locking devices (such as wedges and locking pins) and are designed to different specifications, which makes it difficult and sometimes dangerous to interchange one system with another. However, the majority of systems are made from standard diameter tubes so that they can be used with standard scaffold fittings.

It is vital that specific instruction, training and, where appropriate, an erection plan are provided for the employees erecting any system scaffold. Users should pay strict attention to loading and to the methods of erection published in the manufacturer's or supplier's instructions. There is no national or common specification for system scaffolds. Consequently, care should be taken **not** to mix different systems.

Common types of system scaffold

Some systems are composed of standards with preformed connectors welded at intervals along their length to which ledgers are fixed with a proprietary clamping or wedging arrangement, as shown in Fig. 18.1.

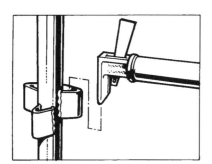
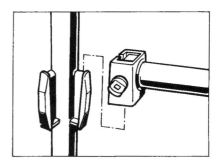
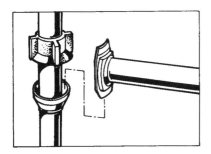
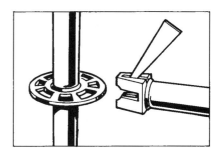

Fig. 18.1

Aluminium components

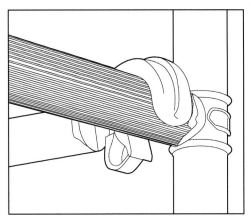

Fig. 18.2

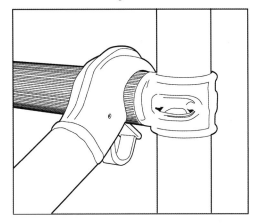

Fig. 18.3

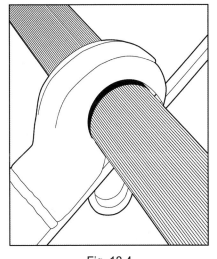

Fig. 18.4

Some earlier systems use tubes made into frames – typically H or X shape, to avoid the need for bracing (Fig. 18.5).

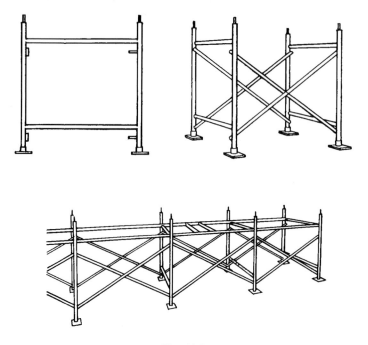

Fig. 18.5

Height of guard-rails

Some existing prefabricated sections, when assembled, will set the top guard-rail at less then the required 950 mm, and so suitable arrangements will need to be made to ensure that the top guard-rail meets the requirement of the Work at Height Regulations.

Components

Standards come in a variety of lengths and have preformed connectors welded at equal distances along their length. A spigot arrangement is formed at one end of the standard for extension purposes; occasionally sockets are found instead.

Ledgers are in varying lengths with connectors welded to each end. The connection is made when the wedge, cup or bolt is hammered or screwed tight.

Transoms are generally made to receive four or five boards. The ends of the transoms are connected to the standards in the same way as the ledgers. Some systems accommodate traditional scaffold boards and therefore require intermediate transoms.

Braces in each direction are made to fit the different bay sizes. Some systems use standard tubes and fittings for bracing.

Boards also called stagings or battens, come in a variety of lengths, thicknesses and widths. Decking is seldom interchangeable as each type is designed to sit exactly on the narrow lip of the transom. Boards are often made from steel with a slip-resistant surface and pre-drilled drainage holes. These systems allow for the attachment of proprietary toe-boards.

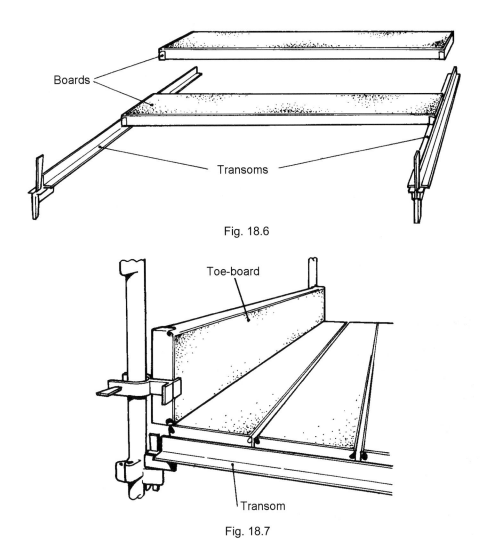

Fig. 18.6

Fig. 18.7

Ties are generally formed in tube and fittings. As yet no one has designed a successful 'system tie'.

Adjustable base plates are essential except on completely level surfaces. In practice, these are often interchangeable between systems. However, care should be taken to establish whether the adjustable base plate is designed for heavy or light-duty use and, where necessary, the SWL (safe working load).

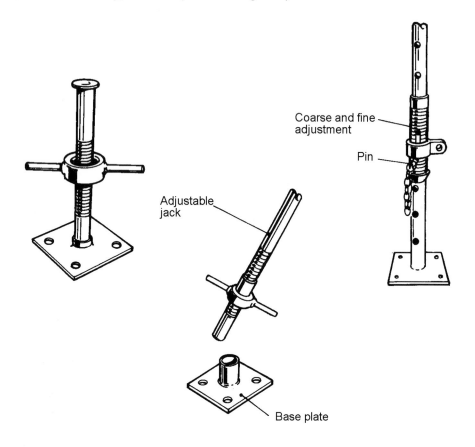

Coarse and fine adjustment

Pin

Adjustable jack

Base plate

Fig. 18.8

Erection methods

1. The foundations are prepared as for other types of scaffold by placing sole boards on firm ground or timber sleepers or, for long-term scaffolds or falsework, by bedding them in a lean concrete mix. Clearly, the type of foundation will depend on the purpose for which the scaffold is intended.

    Sloping or uneven ground can cause problems. Careful consideration should be given to the scaffold's starting point. Setting out should start from the highest point, and adjustable base plates should be used to level the structure.

2. Position the base plate and/or adjustable base plates/jacks in roughly the correct place.

3. Lay out the transoms and ledgers for the first bay so they are ready to fix after the standards are in place.

4. Place a pair of standards on two adjustable base plates and loosely fix the bottom transom.

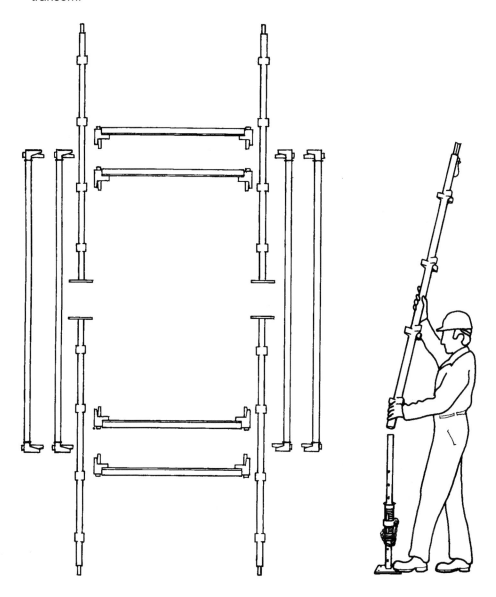

Fig. 18.9

133

5. Fix the transom at head height or above to form a frame.

6. Fix the ledger and third standard.

7. Complete the bay and adjust the jacks to ensure that the bottom ledgers and transoms are level.

8. Tighten up the wedges/fixing attachments.

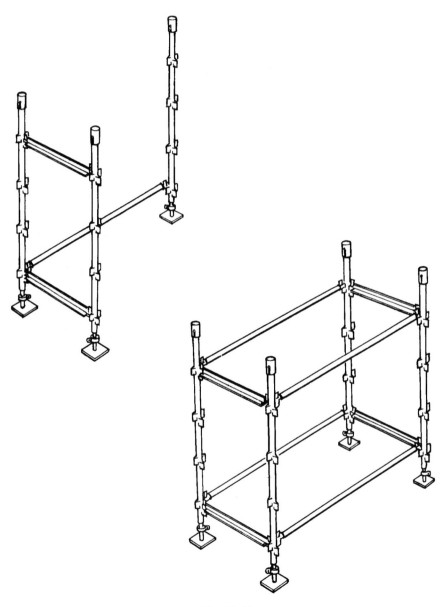

Fig. 18.10

9. Deck out as necessary, and fit temporary guard-rails before erecting subsequent bays and lifts as required.

10. Complete to working lift, deck out and fix the guard-rail and toe-boards, braces and ties as required.

11. Where returns are necessary, careful planning is required to ensure the scaffold 'fits'. This should be done at the first-lift stage.

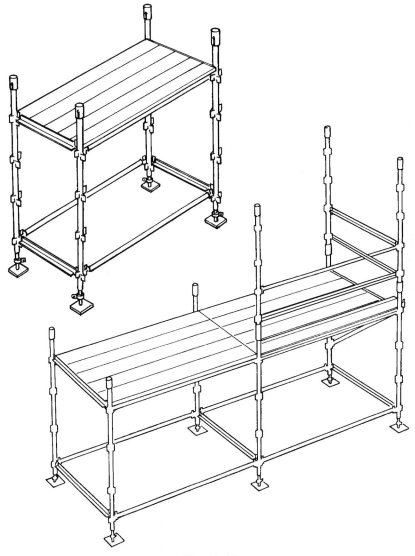

Fig. 18.11

135

Most manufacturers or suppliers produce their own literature describing the erection and dismantling procedures and this should always be referred to. Managers must ensure that the system is suitable for the work, and that employees who are going to erect or assemble system scaffolds are competent to do so and are aware of the basic scaffolding rules, particularly those concerning foundations, bracing, platforms (including guard-rails and toe-boards) and ties.

Health and safety at work

Whatever system of scaffold is used, it is essential that all operatives, regardless of their skill and experience should have regard to their own safety and the safety of others. This is particularly important when system scaffolds are erected as it is by definition 'work at height'. In these cases careful supervision is even more important and supervisors will need to have a sound knowledge of basic scaffolding techniques and the Work at Height Regulations if accidents are to be avoided.

Readers are recommended to study *Safety at Work* (GE 702) – a ConstructionSkills' publication intended primarily for young people entering the construction industry for the first time, but also of value to adult workers and to all those engaged in their supervision and training.

GLOSSARY OF TERMS

Abnormal facade. A facade which does not permit the fixing of through ties or non-movable ties.

Adjustable base plate. A metal base plate embodying a screwjack.

Adjustable forkhead. A forkhead fitted with a threaded spindle and nut to give adjustable height.

Advanced guard-rail. A temporary guard-rail positioned from below while erecting a scaffold.

Anchorage. Component cast or fixed into the building for the purpose of attaching a tie.

Anchor – guy. A pin or tube driven into the ground at approximately 45° to the horizontal to provide an anchorage for a rope.

Base lift. See foot lift.

Base plate. A metal plate with a spigot for distributing the load from a standard or a raker or other load-bearing tube.

Bay. The space between two adjacent standards along the face of a scaffold.

Bay length. The distance between the centres of two adjacent standards, measured horizontally.

Birdcage scaffold. A scaffold structure of a grid of such things as standards and transoms to support a working platform, usually inside a building.

Board – clip. A clip for fixing a board to a scaffold tube.

Board – inside. A board placed between the scaffold and the building on extended transoms, or a hop-up bracket.

Board – retaining. See brick guard.

Board – scaffold. A softwood board combined with others to form access and working platforms and generally used for protective components (such as toe-boards) on a scaffold.

Bolted tie. An assembly of nuts, bolts, anchors, rings or tubes fixed into the surface of a building.

Box tie. An assembly of tubes and couplers forming a tie for the scaffold by enclosing a feature such as a column.

Brace. A tube placed diagonally with respect to the vertical or horizontal members of a scaffold and fixed to them to afford stability.

Brace – facade or face. A brace parallel to the face of a building.

Brace – knee. A brace across the corner of an opening in a scaffold to stiffen the angles or to stiffen the end support of a beam.

Brace – ledger or cross. A brace at right angles to the building.

Brace – longitudinal. A brace in the plane of the longer dimension of the scaffold, particularly in birdcages.

Brace – plan. A brace in a horizontal plane.

Brace – transverse. A brace in the plane of the shorter dimension of the scaffold.

Bracket – hop-up or extension. A bracket attached (usually to the inside of a scaffold) to enable boards to be placed between the scaffold and the building.

Brick guard. (retaining boards)
A barrier, usually of coarse mesh, filling the gap between the guard-rail and the toe-board, and sometimes incorporating one or both of these components.

Bridle. A horizontal tube fixed across an opening or parallel to the face of a building to support the inner end of a putlog transom or tie tube.

Bridle – inside or outside. A bridle either inside or outside a building wall.

Bridle – vertical. A vertical tube performing the same function as a bridle.

Butting transoms. A transom extended inwards to butt the building to prevent the scaffolding moving towards the building.

Butt tube. A short length of tube.

Butting tube. A tube which butts up against the facade of a building or other surface to prevent the scaffold moving towards that surface.

Castor. A swivelling wheel secured to the base of a vertical member for the purpose of mobilising the scaffold.

Check coupler or safety coupler.
A coupler added to a joint under load to give security to the coupler(s) carrying the load.

Chord. The principal longitudinal member(s) of a beam or truss.

Chord stiffener. A tube fixed at right angles to the chord of a prefabricated rafter, beam or truss for the purpose of preventing buckling.

Coupler – fixed finial. A coupler to fix a tube across the end of another at right angles in the same plane, as in the guard-rails.

Coupler – parallel. A coupler used to join two tubes in parallel.

Coupler – purlin, rafter or ridge.
Special angle or variable angle couplers for joining members in sheeted buildings and roofs.

Coupler – putlog. A coupler used for fixing a putlog or transom to a ledger, or to connect a tube used only as a guard-rail to a standard.

Coupler – right-angle. A coupler used to join tubes at right angles.

Coupler – sleeve. An external coupler used to join one tube to another coaxially.

Coupler – supplementary. Coupler(s) added to a joint to back up the main coupler taking the load when the estimated load on the joint is in excess of the safe working load of the main coupler.

Coupler – swivel finial. A coupler to fix a tube across the end of another in the same plane but at an angle, as the handrail to a staircase.

Crane – jib. A small crane specially adapted for pivotal mounting to a scaffold tube.

Cross brace. See ledger brace.

Debris netting. Small mesh netting to catch debris.

Decking. The board(s) or units forming the working platform.

Dowel pin. See spigot pin.

End guard-rail. A guard-rail placed across the end of a scaffold or used to isolate an unboarded part.

End toe-board. A toe-board at the end of a scaffold or at the end of a boarded portion of it.

End toe-board clip. A similar device to the toe-board clip for use on end toe-boards.

Expanding spigot. A device design to expand and grip the inside of a tube. Used for joining tubes.

Facade – abnormal. A facade that does not permit the fixing of through ties or non-movable ties.

Facade brace. Face brace. A brace parallel to the face of a building.

Facade normal. A facade that permits the fixing of through ties or non-movable ties.

Fittings. A general term embracing components other than couplers.

Foot lift. A lift erected near to the ground.

Forkhead. A U-shaped housing for assembly on the end of a tube to accept bearers.

Forkhead – rocking or swivel. A forkhead to accept bearers at a range of angles.

Gin wheel or block. A single pulley for fibre ropes attached to a scaffold for raising or lowering materials.

Going. The horizontal distance between the nosings of two consecutive steps of a stair measured in a horizontal line.

Guard-rail. A member incorporated into a structure to prevent the fall of a person from a platform or access way.

Guard-rail – end. A guard-rail placed across the end of a scaffold or used to isolate an unboarded part.

Guard-rail post. A vertical tube, frequently a puncheon supporting a guard-rail.

Guy anchor. A pin or tube driven into the ground at approximately 45° to the horizontal to provide an anchorage for a rope.

Height. The height measured from the foundation to the top assembly of ledgers and transoms.

Hop-up or extension bracket. A bracket attached to the inside of a scaffold to enable boards to be placed between the scaffold and the building.

Independent tied scaffold. A scaffold that has two lines of standards, one line supporting the outside of the deck and one the inside. The transoms are not built into the wall of the building. It is not free-standing, but relies on the building for stability.

Inside board. A board placed between the scaffold and the building on extended transoms, or on hop-up brackets.

Interlock pin. See spigot pin.

Jib crane. A small crane specially adapted for pivotal mounting to a scaffold tube.

Joint pin. An expanding fitting placed in the bore of a tube to connect one tube to another coaxially (see spigot).

Kentledge. A dead-weight built up or added to a structure to ensure adequate stability.

Ledger. A longitudinal tube normally fixed parallel to the face of a building in the direction of the larger dimensions of the scaffold. It acts as a support for the putlogs and transoms and frequently for tie tubes and ledger braces, and is fixed to the adjacent standards.

Ledger or cross brace. A brace at right angles to the building.

Lift. The assembly of ledgers and transoms forming each horizontal level of a scaffold.

Lift – foot. A lift erected near to the ground.

Lift head room. The clear distance between a platform and the tubular assembly of the lift above.

Light height. The vertical distance between two lifts, measured centre to centre.

Lip tie. An assembly of tubes forming an L or J-shaped hook round a part of a building.

Lip tie – double. A lip tie that is a push/pull tie (i.e. has a cross tube on the back and front of the wall).

Longitudinal brace. A brace in the plane of the longer dimension of the scaffold, particularly in birdcages.

Movable ties. A tie that may be temporarily moved for the execution of work.

Needle transom. A transom extending into or out of a building.

Node. Point where two scaffold members are connected together.

Normal facade. A facade that permits the fixing of through ties and non-movable ties.

Parallel coupler. A coupler used to joint two tubes in parallel.

Plan brace. A brace in a horizontal plane, often diagonally between front and back standards.

Prop tie. An assembly of telescopic props and/or scaffold tube jacked or wedged between the floors of a storey inside a building and including a tie tube.

Puncheon. A vertical tube supported at its lower end by another scaffold tube or beam and not by the ground or on a deck.

Purlin. A tube secured to the rafters of a building and parallel to the ridge for the purpose of attaching the roof covering and to act as a top chord stiffener for the rafter beams.

Push/pull tie. A tie that acts to prevent the scaffold moving either towards or away from the building (e.g. a reveal tie, a box tie, a double lip tie or a bolted tie with a tie tube).

Putlog. A tube with a blade or flattened end, to rest in or on part of the brickwork or structure.

Putlog adaptor. A fitting to provide a putlog blade on the end of scaffold tube.

Putlog coupler. A coupler used for fixing a putlog or transom to a ledger, or to connect a tube used only as a guard-rail to a standard.

Rafter and rafter beam. A transverse tube, beam or truss in a building spanning across a roof or from the eaves to the ridge.

Raker. An inclined load-bearing tube.

Retaining bar. A strip or device fixed across the top of the decking to hold it down.

Retaining boards. See brick guard.

Reveal screw pin. A fitting used for tightening a reveal tube between two opposing surfaces.

Reveal tie. The assembly of a reveal tube with wedges or screwed fittings, and pads, if required, fixed between opposing faces of an opening in a wall together with the tie tube.

Reveal tube. A tube fixed by means of a threaded fitting or by wedging between two opposing surfaces of a structure (e.g. between two window reveals to form an anchor to which the scaffolding may be tied).

Right-angle coupler. A coupler used to join tubes at right angles.

Rise. The vertical distance between two steps of a stair.

Roofing clip or sheeting clip. A fitting for fixing roof or wall sheeting to tubes in structures without the need for holes in the sheeting.

Safe Working Load (SWL). The maximum load that should be imposed on a scaffold or working platform.

Scaffold. A temporary structure that provides access, or from which persons work, or that is used to support materials, plant or equipment.

Scaffold board. A softwood board combined with others to form access and working platforms and that is generally used for protective components such as toe-boards on a scaffold.

Scaffold – free-standing. A scaffold that is not attached to any other structure but is stable in itself or, if necessary, stabilised by rakers and/or anchors.

Scaffold – independent tied. A scaffold that has two lines of standards, one line supporting the outside of the deck and one the inside. The transoms are not built into the wall of the building. It is not free-standing, but relies on the building for stability.

Scaffold – putlog. A scaffold that has one line of standards to support the outside edge of the deck and utilises the wall being built or the building to support the inside edge.

Scaffold – slung. A scaffold hanging on tubes, ropes or chains from a structure overhead. It is not capable of being moved or lowered.

Scaffold – suspended. A scaffold hanging on ropes that is capable of being raised and lowered.

Sheeting. Horizontal, vertical or inclined sheets of material, such as corrugated metal or plastic sheet, attached to a scaffold in order to provide protection from the effects of weather or alternatively to protect the surrounding area from the effects of works being carried out from the scaffold structure.

Sheeting hook. A threaded rod hook with a washer and a nut used for attaching sheeting to tubes.

Sheeting rail. A horizontal tube fixed to the verticals of a scaffold to support the sheeting.

Sill. See sole plate.

Skirt. A short portion of vertical sheeting usually adjacent to the edge of a roof to give extra protection to the area enclosed immediately under the roof.

Sleeve coupler. An external coupler used to join one tube to another coaxially.

Sole board or sole plate. A timber, concrete or metal spreader used to distribute the load from a standard or base plate to the ground.

Spigot. An internal fitting to join one tube to another coaxially (see joint pin).

Spigot – expanding. A device designed to expand and grip the inside of a tube. Used for joining tubes.

Spigot pin. A pin placed transversely through the spigot and the scaffold tube to prevent the two from coming apart.

Spine beam. A longitudinal main beam spanning from end to end of a roof at the ridge or eaves.

Standard. A vertical or near-vertical tube.

Standards – pair of. The standards forming the frame at right angles to the building.

Supplementary coupler. Coupler(s) added to a joint to back up the main coupler taking the load when the estimated load on the joint is in excess of the safe working load of the main coupler.

Sway transom. A transom extended inwards in contact with a reveal or the side of a column to prevent the scaffold moving sideways.

Swivel coupler. A coupler used for joining tubes at an angle other than a right angle.

Swivel finial coupler. A coupler to fix a tube across the end of another in the same plane but at an angle, as the handrail to a staircase.

Tension pin. See spigot pin.

Tie tube. A tube used to connect a scaffold to an anchorage.

Tie or tie assembly. The components attached to an anchorage or the building or framed around a part of it or wedged or screwed into it. Used with a tie tube to secure the scaffold to the structure.

Tie – bolted. An assembly of nuts, bolts, anchors, rings or tubes fixed to the surface of a building.

Tie – box. An assembly of tubes and couplers forming a tie for the scaffold by enclosing a feature such as a column.

Tie – double lip. A lip tie that is a push/pull tie (i.e. has a cross tube on the back and front of the wall).

Tie – lip. An assembly of tubes forming an L or J shaped hook round part of a building.

Tie – movable. A tie that may be temporarily moved for the execution of work.

Tie-prop. An assembly of telescopic props and/or scaffold tube jacked or wedged between the floors of a storey inside a building and including a tie tube.

Tie – push/pull. A tie that acts to prevent the scaffold moving either towards or away from the building (e.g. a reveal tie, a box tie, a double lip tie or a bolted tie with a tie tube).

Tie – reveal. The assembly of a reveal tube with wedges or screwed fittings and pads, if required, fixed between opposing faces of an opening in a wall together with the tie tube.

Tie – through. A tie assembly through a window or other opening in a wall.

Tie – wire or band. An assembly of a ring anchor and wire or steel banding used to tie the scaffold to the building.

Toe-board. An upstand normally at the outer edge of a platform intended to prevent materials or operative's feet from slipping off the platform.

Toe-board clip. A clip used for attaching toe-boards to tubes.

Toe-board – end. A toe-board at the end of a scaffold or at the end of a boarded portion of it.

Toe-board – end clip. A similar device to the toe-board clip for use on end toe-boards.

Transom. A tube to connect the outer standards to the inner standards or spanning across ledgers to form the support for boards or units forming the working platform.

Transoms – butting. A transom extended inwards to butt the building to prevent the scaffolding moving towards the building.

Transom – needle. A transom extended from or into a building.

Transom – sway. A transom extended inwards in contact with a reveal or the side of a column to prevent the scaffold moving sideways.

Vertical bridle. A vertical tube performing the same function as a bridle.

Width. The width of a scaffold measured at right angles to the ledgers from centre to centre of the upright. Sometimes designated by the number of boards within the uprights and the number beyond the uprights on extended transoms.

Working load. The load a structural member can carry having regard to the conditions.

Working platform. The deck from which building operations are carried out.

INDEX